MW00452494

Paid in Sunsets

A Park Ranger's Story

By David. A. Dutton

Culicidae
PRESS, LLC
culicidaepress.com

Ames | Gainesville | Lemgo | Rome

Culicidae Press, LLC
922 5th Street
Ames, IA 50010
USA
www.culicidaepress.com
editor@culicidaepress.com

Ames | Gainesville | Lemgo | Rome

PAID IN SUNSETS: A PARK RANGER'S STORY.

Copyright © 2016 by David A. Dutton. All rights reserved.

No part of this book may be reproduced in any form by any electronic or mechanized means (including photocopying, recording, or information stor- age and retrieval) without written permission, except in the case of brief quotations embodied in critical articles and reviews.
For more information, please visit www.culicidaepress.com

ISBN-13:   978-1-941892-30-5

ISBN-10:   1-941892-30-2

Cover design and interior layout © 2016 by polytekton.com
Sunset photos on cover by Mary B. Dutton

To Kate
Who taught me to never give up

Table of Contents

Acknowledgements

When someone suggests that you should write a book, you have options: run like hell the other way, or pick up a pen and paper. I chose the later, but not without considerable urging. If it were not for the encouragement of my wife Mary B to write a book about my rangering yarns, it might never have become a reality. Same goes for my son Logan, who freely offered millennial input, and when the time came, stepped up and cared for his old man.

Thanks also to other family members, all of whom endured the telling and retelling of Ranger stories at family get-togethers; brother Tom—your advice was always collegiate, always salient; brother Paul, a working man—your real-life perspectives were always encouraging, and Mom, who, at two years shy of being a nonagenarian, reminded me at every turn, "David, I'd like to read the book before I die." No pressure there.

Colleagues Nancy Rogers, Rebecca Miner and Vance Austin, Park Rangers all, are owed a debt of gratitude for their insights and observations when the manuscript was in its infancy, and who helped me to keep the narrative grounded.

This book certainly would not have come to fruition without the guiding hand of Lauren Camp—accomplished poet and artist. Her wisdom, unfailing patience and uncanny ability to gently peel band aids off of bad writing, helped me to keep going, even when I didn't want to.

Lastly, a shout out to all Park Rangers across this land— men and women who put on a uniform and step into the crowd to bolster the ranks of the Thin Green Line—you are the unsung heroes!

Thin Green Line

Some national parks have long waiting lists for camping reservations. When you have to wait a year to sleep next to a tree, something is wrong.
~ George Carlin

I was a Park Ranger once. For thirty-one years. Everyday I put on a uniform and a big hat, stepped into the crowd, and reinforced an ideal—what Rangers refer to as the "thin green line"—ensuring America's treasures are protected and enjoyed for future generations.

Park Rangers are emblematic of many things—ruggedness, individualism, courage. They're called upon to do dangerous things, like rappel down cliff faces to rescue stranded climbers, or cut fire lines in advance of raging forest fires. I didn't do those things; what I did was share the natural world with others.

Somewhere in my memory archives, maybe when I was six years old, I remember a family vacation to Grand Teton National Park. I recall sleeping in a battered pup tent along with my older brother Tom, and having to go pee in the middle of a cold night. I walked bare-footed to the outhouse, cursing every pointy Lodgepole pinecone I stepped on. Trembling in cotton PJ's, I vented into a porcelain trough mounted along a wall. Outside the kibo, garbage cans were being savaged by bears. *Why didn't I just piss outside the tent?* I sprinted back (pinecones be damned), torpedoed into my sleeping bag, and shivered my way to warmth, exhilarated and scared at the same time. The next day, I told a

Park Ranger about my experience. He took a knee, put a strong hand on my shoulder, and told me to be careful around bears.

When I was about to enter junior high school, my family moved to Shadow Hills—a modest, middle class enclave in the east end of the San Fernando Valley—where houses, horse corrals and flies coexisted. My curiosity for the natural world intensified. I collected bugs of every imaginable variety and color, as well as spiders, snakes, lizards (especially the Paleozoic-looking alligator lizards), worms, pupae, toads…whatever I could find. Some of the beasties I put in glass jars with lids (always with holes for air). After a little while, I'd let them go.

One summer morning, I foisted a writhing Gopher snake on Mom. I knew it wasn't a rattlesnake, but she might have thought otherwise. The snake's beautiful cream and dark diamond markings are strikingly similar to a rattlesnake's. No matter. Mom shrieked and shrieked. I knew snakes didn't have ears, which is probably why it seemed unfazed by the ordeal. I released the snake in a field below our house—what Dad called "the lower forty"—and caught him again a few years later. Absent kinks, he was taller than our front door. After I joined the Army, Mom wrote me and said the snake had been *accidentally* run over by our neighbor, Mr. Nelson, as it lay stretched across his driveway adjacent to the lower forty. I never forgave Mr. Nelson for it.

In high school, Mr. Comoletti, our assistant football coach, and a man who unfailingly wore a white golf cap, talked to our health class about his summers as a Park Ranger at Yosemite. I was intrigued by his exploits. It started me thinking: How great it would be to live and work in the outdoors?

Following a brief stint in the US Army, I returned home with a plan. I enrolled in the Natural Resources Management program at California Polytechnic State University, San Luis Obispo. For my entrance essay, I wrote that becoming a Park Ranger was encoded in my DNA. I'm guessing the selection board liked that. In the spring of 1978, I packed my bags and said goodbye to sleepy Shadow Hills.

At the time, the Natural Resources Management (NRM) program at Cal Poly was in its infancy. It was coupled with the School of Agriculture, seemingly as an afterthought. It may have looked something like this:

School of Agriculture
and Natural Resources

During my freshman year, I took an animal parasitology course. The classroom resembled a sheep pen with desks, and smelled like a petting zoo. The instructor started off by asking the class their respective fields of study.

"Show of hands," he asked, "how many of you are bovine?"

Veterinarians study cows, but these folks didn't look veterinary. They were the sons and daughters of farmers and ranchers, who would return home after getting an education, and manage large agribusinesses. I was a suburban kid who wanted to be a Park Ranger. The inquisition continued.

"Equine?" A spattering of hands rose up, although the pool was steadily shrinking.

"Ovis?" A few tepid hands more.

"Sus?"

After he'd exhausted his barnyard list, he turned to me and asked: "Sir, you didn't raise your hand. Why not?"

"I'm an NRM major," I answered, proudly.

"Oh, you're one of them."

As "one of them," I quickly became immersed in every imaginable "ology"—mammalogy, ornithology, herpetology, plant ecology, dendrology, plus a boatload more. I often wondered—after spending three hours in an Entomology lab trying to key out a species of leafhopper—how this would help me become a Park Ranger, but I persevered.

Just before completing my sophomore year in the spring of 1980, I dropped by my faculty adviser's office. I needed guidance on how to break into the field of Rangering. My résumé was anorexic—grocery store bagger, horseshit shoveler, deputy assistant afterschool playground attendant, butcher, baker—these weren't exactly the experiences that land you Park Ranger jobs. My adviser, a stylish academian with plaid pants, a bowtie and saddle shoes, suggested I apply for a position with the Student Conservation Association, an organization specializing in hands-on environmental stuff.

"Federal agencies work them like mules," he said. "Kind of a cheap labor force. In exchange you get some valuable outdoor experience. And they'll even pay you five dollars a day!" He handed me a pamphlet.

"Five dollars a day?" *That's doable if I cut down on beer.*

I took the SCA application home to my apartment, complete with a dying ficus, paper thin walls and orange shag carpet, and began writing. A month later, I received a phone call from a nice lady at SCA Headquarters. I'd been accepted at Bandelier National Monument—a National Park Service outpost in the Jemez Mountains of northern New Mexico. I thanked the lady and hung up the phone.

I popped a beer from the fridge, found a dated atlas, and sat down at the kitchen table. New Mexico? I pictured Wylie Coyote baying atop buff-colored mesas, steely-eyed sidewinders slaloming through dunes of white sand, and lots and lots of prickly cacti.

#

It's 1,041 miles from San Luis Obispo, California, to Bandelier National Monument, New Mexico, not counting the half-mile detour I made to the Cork 'n' Bottle liquor store to stock up on the best road food of all time—corn nuts. I stuffed my '63 VW Bug—which was only three colors, if you didn't count the gray bondo—with everything I figured I needed for three months. I'd be joining legions of idealistic SCA neophytes fanning out across the nation, all eager for a career opportunity in the great outdoors.

By late afternoon on my first day, I'd made it to Barstow, California. I gassed up, and bought a Sony Walkman and a Billy Joel cassette at Radio Shack. Some asshole had stolen my prized Blaupunkt AM/FM stereo when I stopped in Bakersfield. The theft left an unsightly hole in the dash, which I covered with silver duct tape. Next up, Needles, California—a furnace-like stopover on the western banks of the Colorado River—internationally recognized for setting world record temperatures. *No AC, no cruise control…but hey, I have the Piano Man on the boom box.*

By early evening, the Bug and I struggled to reach the top of the Kaibab Plateau. I pulled off the interstate in Flagstaff, Arizona, and into a gravel parking lot that fronted a log cabin with a flashing neon Hamm's Beer sign in the front window. I went inside and ordered one. The place hummed with a collegiate vibe, and smelled of spilled hops, sweat and perfume. I'd not factored a hotel stay into my meager travel budget. Gas, corn nuts and a Walkman were about it. I asked several coeds where I could camp.

"Anywhere," they said. "Just pull off the road, and camp under the pines. Everyone does it."

I washed down a greasy burger with another icy Hamm's, and set out in search of a place to bed down for the night. A half-hour later I was hopelessly lost on a dark road, looking for anywhere to lay out a sleeping bag. Powered only by a six-volt battery, the Bug's headlights were no match for the inky pitch of the Kaibab forest. The ascending road truncated, and I turned in. Headlights shined on a small patch of grass. *This will do nicely.*

I spread out a tarp, draped my sweaty clothes over a nearby post, and slithered into my sleeping bag. Lying cocooned in goose down, I stared up at our galaxy. At 7,000 feet above sea level, the Big Dipper seemed close enough to grab its' handle. The next day, if everything went well, I'd be at Bandelier National Monument.

Get Off My Lawn!

*To me a lush carpet of pine needles or spongy grass is
more welcome than the most luxurious Persian rug*
~ Helen Keller

The next morning, I was awakened by a deep voice.

"Son, you can't camp here."

Curled deep in my warm mummy bag, I barely heard the voice. He poked at my sleeping bag like it was road kill.

"You aren't allowed to camp here. This is government housing. Did you miss the sign?" the voice asked.

I surfaced for air and squinted at the stranger kneeling next to me. He wore a wide-brimmed hat that blocked the morning sun. His clean shaven face was weather-worn. He smiled down at me. It was a warm, disarming smile, the kind a Little League coach might use after one of his kid's strikes out for the fourth time. I sensed he unleashed it lot, probably on gypsy campers like me. My head throbbed. I fumbled for my water bottle in the dewy grass. Cool water loosened my tongue.

"I'm sorry, sir. I didn't know," I said, from behind a dripping moustache.

"Well, you'll need to collect your things and move on."

I watched him stride across the glistening lawn. He wore gray and green—the colors of a National Park Service Ranger. His Smokey the Bear hat fit perfectly atop his head. I was about to tell him I was bound for Bandelier National Monument for a summer job, but didn't. *No use making waves, Dutton.* He got into his truck, flashed another hearty smile, and drove away.

I sat up and looked around. From the cozy confines of my bag, I saw a row of neat little houses. I hadn't seen them when I abruptly pulled in last night. The Park Ranger that woke me up probably lived in one of them. I'd practically camped on his front lawn.

Although it was early June, the high altitude air still had a nip to it. Pinyon jays sang their trademark solos from perches high in nearby Ponderosa trees. I squirmed out of my sleeping bag and stretched. *Where are my clothes?*

Turning around, I eyed them—Levi cut-offs, plaid boxers, T-shirt—all hung limply on a wooden sign with perfectly white, routed letters, which read:

GOVERNMENT HOUSING
NO CAMPING

I tiptoed across the wet grass and put them on. My boxers were still dank, and shot chills up my groin. I had to pee, but lifting a leg on the nice Ranger's lawn wouldn't do. I cocooned my down bag, tossed it in the Bug, and set off in search of a strong cup of coffee.

With the Bug's heater warming my ankles, I drove north on a spur road, until it ended at the interstate. I glanced over my shoulder. A rock entrance sign read:

Walnut Canyon
National Monument
Open 8AM - 6PM

I drove west on I-40, back toward Flagstaff, and exited onto a frontage road to piss, gas, and eat. I pulled into a Ma & Pa convenience store, and went inside. The place reeked of cigarettes, coffee, and corn dogs. I asked the man behind the counter—a bearded goliath with a T-shirt that read *Gun Control Means Using*

Both Hands—how far it was to Gallup. He turned and studied a faded Route 66 map tacked to a paneled wall. A colorful tattoo of a grinning skeleton wrapped in a confederate flag adorned his thick neck. He smelled like Old Milwaukee leftover in a Solo cup. Finally, he rested his hairy forearms on the counter, drew deeply on a Marlboro, and exhaled through his nose.

"That's about a two six-pack drive."

It wasn't quite 8:00 in the morning according to the Coca-Cola wall clock above the Slurpee machine. *Little early for a Bud, don't you think?*

"Nice tattoo," I said, grabbing a package of powdered donuts.

I poured coffee into a Styrofoam cup, mashed on the lid and laid five dollars on the counter. The man punched the keys on an antique cash register like it was Whack-a-mole, until a drawer flew open and slammed into his belly.

"Sir, do you have a restroom?" I asked.

The piss-o-meter was pegging PISS OR DIE. Old Milwaukee eyed me suspiciously, taking in my shoulder length hair, Los Angeles Lakers T-shirt, Levi cut-offs, Nike shoes, and no socks. *Yeah, I'm a hippie, but a polite one.* He reached under the counter and handed me an oversized key attached to an oversized metal ring that was duct-taped to an oversized broom handle.

"Roun' back," he said, motioning to the rear of the building.

"Thanks." I grabbed the broom handle and headed for the back of the building.

"Don't fuck anything up!" he shouted to my back.

I put six bucks of regular—what my Aunt Mayme called "ethyl,"—in the Bug, and rocked it gently. I cocked an ear to the tank, listening for the swishing sounds of gas. *That outta get me to Gallup.*

I climbed in the Bug, engaged the interstate, and pulled behind an eighteen wheeler, taking advantage of its draft like a goose in formation. I popped a donut into my mouth, spewing sugary whiteness all over the Lakers. With my right hand on the wheel and my left arm half bent out the window, I looked out on monotonous flatlands and far-off mesas—the iconic topography of the Basin and Range Province of the Great Southwest. Geologists think the earth's crust is so stretched in this part of the Southwest, it's considered the thinnest in the world.

A whistling Billy Joel blasted from the Sony Walkman sitting on the passenger seat. I reached for my coffee, and took a sip. It was vile. I almost threw the damn cup out the window, but a bug-eyed Woodsy the Owl—an icon of the 1970's environmental movement—appeared like a hologram, angrily pointing his long pipe at me. *Give a Hoot Don't Pollute!* Growing up, I was taught if you litter, your hair will fall out. For the next fifty miles, I drank the swill, glad for the buzz, and tossed the empty cup onto the passenger-side floorboard, along with the other road effluvia I'd collected since leaving San Luis Obispo the day before.

As I drove over skinny mantle, my mind drifted back to 1962, and the summer the family journeyed to the Mecca of Boy Scoutdom—Philmont Scout Ranch in northern New Mexico. Dad was a young Boy Scout executive at the time. I was seven. We had a Woody station wagon. From the backseat, I stared out at nothing and more nothing. To alleviate the insane tedium, I began counting brightly colored billboards along Route 66— the Mother Road—which advertised moccasins, Navajo tacos, Indian jewelry, kachinas, clean restrooms, cigs.

My father's approach to traveling was geometrical; the shortest distance between two points meant never stopping. He devised an ingenious way to circumvent pit-stops altogether—a pickle jar. During one interminable stretch, I was full to bust.

"Dad, I really need to peeeeeee!!!!!"

"No problem son, just use the jar."

I climbed over the backseat and placed the glass pickle jar between my knees, swaying with the rhythm of the highway. I evacuated a glorious stream into it. Warm, bubbly liquid splashed over the rim. I put the jar down and climbed back over the seat, wiping my wet hands on my jeans.

"Dad, I don't have to pee no more!"

"That's good, son."

#

Three hours after leaving the Ma & Pa store, and after countless dilapidated billboards, miles of barbed-wire fences, and herds of nomadic, blank-eyed bovine, an exit sign for Gallup appeared. I took it. A black pickup truck closed fast from the opposite direction, weaving like a sidewinder snake. The truck whizzed by, nearly taking my side mirror with it. I yanked the Bug onto the shoulder. Glass bottles exploded under my tires. The pickup zigzagged, then caromed off a light pole and into a steep ditch. With only a sinew of aluminum support, the streetlight toppled to the ground, puking glass and metal across the bypass.

I made a U-turn, pulled alongside the shoulder, got out and looked into the ditch. The truck's radiator hemorrhaged steamy fluids, and acrid smoke billowed from underneath the chassis. An avulsed headlamp, suspended by frayed wires, hung limply against a punched-in grill. Someone inside the cab kicked at the driver's door. A man in a straw cowboy hat and long-sleeved shirt rolled out. He staggered around the hissing vehicle, cursing in Spanish, kicking at the lifeless heap with his pointy cowboy boots. He fumbled for a cigarette in his bloody shirt pocket, lit it, then reached inside the cab and pulled out a six-pack. Sitting on the ditch bank, he struggled with the pull tab. He glanced up at me. Beer suds dripped from his dark moustache. I heard sirens wailing in the distance, and decided I'd better go. Driving into town, I couldn't help but think about what the Neanderthal at the Ma & Pa store in Flagstaff averred—"That's about a two six-pack drive."

Downtown Gallup, with its turn-of-the-century buildings and wooden sidewalks, resembled a movie set for a western. Atchison, Topeka and Santa Fe Railroad flat cars crept slowly through town. Trading posts selling Navajo rugs, turquoise jewelry, and pottery, faced the main drag. The storefronts were connected by a splintered, wooden boardwalk. Hardened men wearing cowboy boots and turquoise leaned against posts outside of bars. The light pole slayer that nearly hit me probably had warmed a barstool at one of them.

I drove farther and found a burger joint on the outskirts of town. Pulling under a canopy, I pressed a red button under the marquee and ordered up. The powdered dounts had long since metabolized, and now I was on the ornery side of a sugar high. The burger joint smelled of deep fried onion rings and meat, and sent my taste buds into overdrive.

"Would you like chile with that cheeseburger?"

Chili on a cheeseburger? Why the hell not? "Yes, please."

A teenage girl with long, lampblack hair and high cheekbones skated up to my car. I paid for my order, peeled back the foil, and ripped a bite.

Holy shit!

My mouth instantly erupted, spewing forth hot mucus. My cheeks felt like the surface of the sun. I groped for my Coke. The cherry-flavored drink did nothing to quench the four-alarm fire in my head. In fact, it made the burning worse. Fervid tears rolled down my face. I coughed, punched the air, and cursed. Families in parked cars next to me cast frightened looks. *I'm going to die in a shitty burger joint in Gallup, New Mexico!* I managed to find the red button under the menu placard. At least I could still see colors.

"Yes, can I help you?"

"Cou'd I pleeees gee a up of ater?" I may have been crying. My lips felt like sandbags. *Try sign language, Dutton.*

"I'll have it right out."

The young girl rolled up again. She smiled and handed me a large cup of ice water.

"Ank ou."

"The green chile is hot today," she said, then skated off for another order.

Green chile? *Chile with an "e", not an "i"* Never again would I transpose those two vowels. I'd never eaten anything so hot in my life, yet it was strangely satisfying. My obsession with chile, and all things hot, really, started with *that* cheeseburger in Gallup, New Mexico.

After the shaking subsided, I backed out and found an on-ramp for Albuquerque. Teary-eyed, I stuck my head out the window. The wind felt plenary rushing past my face, until a semi roared by, and I retracted my head like a tortoise into its shell. I took a long pull of my Cherry Coke. From the passenger seat, Billy J sang about dying young.

#

Late afternoon shadows stretched long across the landscape as the Bug and I chugged up the flanks of an ancient volcano, enroute to Los Alamos, New Mexico. My foot pressed down on my hang-ten gas pedal, pushing the Bug higher and higher into the Jemez Mountains. I gazed out at pinkish, pockmarked rocks that reminded me of Swiss cheese. Later, I learned the rocks were actually compressed volcanic ash known as tuff. In some places it was two football fields thick. The sun felt genial radiating through the windshield, which after two days on the road, was splattered with all manner of insect parts. The sinuous road to Bandelier plunged into deep canyons and skirted panoramic mesas, stubbled with dense stands of Ponderosa pine and juniper. This certainly wasn't the landscape I'd pictured when I found out I'd been accepted as an SCA intern at Bandelier National Monument.

An entrance sign for the monument beckoned up ahead. I drove past an unmanned adobe entrance station. A two-lane blacktop road passed a fire tower and an observation pullout, before making a sweeping arc and dropping into a spectacular canyon with towering tuff walls. Far below I could see the Rio Grande shimmering in the late afternoon sun. At the bottom of the canyon, the road flattened out, emptying into a small, oval parking lot, flanked by angular rock buildings with pointy timbers sticking out near the roof line.

I parked in front of the Visitor Center (VC) and got out. The parking lot was empty. I stretched hard. Overhead, billowy clouds floated through an absurdly blue sky. My Lakers T-shirt was sweat-stained, and carried the reminders of everyplace I'd eaten along the way. Closing my eyes, I inhaled the intoxicating perfumes of juniper and pine. The afternoon sun had exited the canyon, and a cool breeze ruffled through nearby cottonwoods. Crickets chorused in unison. Behind me, a creek splashed and gurgled as it sashayed over rocks. For a broke college sophomore with no girly prospects, Bandelier was a most welcome sight.

I tucked in my shirt, tamed my highway hair in the Bug's side mirror, and walked through the wooden double doors of the VC, looking for someone in a big hat.

Hopefully, tonight, I'd sleep in the right place.

Water Dogs and Canned Beans

Cold morning on Aztec Peak Fire Lookout. First, build fire in old
stove. Second, start coffee. Then, heat up last night's pork chops
and spinach for breakfast. Why not? And why the hell not?
~ Edward Abbey

I spent my first night at Bandelier National Monument in a
fire tower. It wasn't the steel-stilted, stairway-to-heaven
variety, typical of many in the remote forests of the American
West. Rather, Bandelier's fire tower was a two-story stone and
wood structure built in the 1930's by the Civilian Conservation
Corps. From its' perch atop Frijoles Canyon, it commanded a
360 degree view—the Jemez Mountains to the west, Pajarito
Mesa to the North, the Sangre de Cristo Mountains and Santa
Fe to the East, and the highlands of Albuquerque to the South.
The ground floor of the fire tower consisted of a studio-sized
apartment; complete with a small bath, kitchen and bed, while
the top floor served as a lookout, surrounded on all sides by a
wooden plank balcony.

My duty station throughout the summer of 1980 was
Bandelier's Visitor Center, in the heart of Frijoles Canyon. Each
work day, I negotiated a twisty mile and a half trail, dropping
600 feet to the canyon below. In the late afternoon, after my
shift, I hiked back up to the mesa. I learned to guide visitors
through Bandelier's stony Pueblonian ruins, give nature walks
and campfire programs. I was doing what I wanted to do—share
nature with others.

Typically, I spent my evenings sitting on the fire tower's overhanging veranda, eating canned beans (beans were always on sale at the White Rock grocery), enjoying the furnace-orange hues of a New Mexico sunset. Rangers refer to this as, "Paid in Sunsets."

Following the sunset show, came the more ribald after show. Horny, male Common nighthawks—robin-sized, night-dwelling birds—flitted high in the skies over the fire tower. They'd dive steeply, breaking their freefall with their tail feathers, creating a noise remarkably like a boisterous fart. They were attracting mates. I guess female nighthawks liked it. I'd listen, then smile whenever I heard the inevitable "breaking wind."

When twilight gave way to full-on dark, I climbed onto the roof of the fire tower and gazed up at the night sky. Occasionally I was treated to colorful meteors zinging silently through the night sky. *You're livin' the dream, Dutton!*

When the summer monsoons arrived in early July, I was tasked with monitoring lightning strikes from the fire tower. After storms passed, I'd scan the mesas and canyons for signs of smoke. One afternoon, after a particularly virulent storm, multiple smokes swirled up from the canyons below. Dutifully, I radioed in their approximate locations.

"We got a good smoke in southwest Capulin Canyon"... "Smoke rising, upper Frijoles Canyon." Wildfire smoke seemed to be wafting up from every corner of the monument. After about fifteen minutes of frantic spotting, a patrol Ranger pulled up to the fire tower in his truck. No doubt he'd heard my reports coming over the radio. He bounded up the stairs, grabbed the binoculars from my hands, and focused on a smoke in upper Alamo Canyon. After several minutes, he put the binocs down, turned to me, and said, "Those are water dogs, Dutton. They're not wildfires."

He explained that what I was seeing was water vapor which had condensed into spiraling columns after the storm passed, and the sun re-warmed the canyons. I would've sworn in a court of law I was seeing wildfire smoke. He handed me back the binoculars. "Don't feel bad. Everyone here has called in a water dog or two," he reassured.

#

One of the things I enjoyed most about working in the VC was interacting with visitors. People from around the world came to Bandelier to marvel at the ingenuity, resourcefulness, and architectural prowess of the Anasazi—the ones who centuries before, eked out a living in Frijoles canyon, and who unexpectedly left behind the stony remnants of their culture.

The other thing I enjoyed about my job was working with Mrs. Evelyn Frey—the Lady of the Canyon. When I first met her, she sat cross-legged on a stool in the VC talking about her life in Frijoles Canyon. She wore a plum-colored jacket and matching skirt, and had red, short-bobbed hair. Her eyes sparkled from behind horn-rimmed glasses as she talked. Families sat about, hanging on every word. Mrs. Frey was a born storyteller.

Through eleven presidential administrations—from "Silent Cal" in the 1920s to "The Gipper" in the 1980s—Mrs. Frey had toughed out a living between the tuff walls of Frijoles Canyon. Only the ancient Anasazi had lived in the canyon longer than she. Mrs. Frey also had a pioneer concessionaire heritage. She'd managed a guest ranch in Frijoles Canyon after Bandelier National Monument was officially designated in 1916. Back then, the only way in and out of the canyon was via the Frey Trail. I would become familiar with every switchback of it during my walks to and from the fire tower.

When the National Park Service took over control of her guest ranch in 1932, Mrs. Frey became the chief head-knocker of the Frijoles Canyon Lodge, which was built by CCC workers. During World War II, Mrs. Frey hobnobbed with men like Robert Oppenheimer and General Leslie Groves—icons of the Manhattan Project.

Mrs. Frey was also a gifted palm reader, and often asked if she could read mine. She cradled my palm in her soft, wrinkled hands, adjusted her horn-rimmed glasses, and scrutinized it like a cryptologist. She was never quite comfortable with my bachelor status, and although she'd studied my palm many times before, she remained hopeful there'd be something new.

One day, toward the end of summer, Mrs. Frey surprised me with a gift—a Hopi good luck ring. It had an open spiral design, which in the Hopi culture, denotes broadened consciousness. She placed the ring in my palm, and whispered in my ear, "You'll find someone special."

I wanted to believe her. But where would I find someone willing to share a fire tower with?

#

After my summer SCA stint, I pocketed the Hopi ring and headed back to Cal Poly to start my junior year. I arrived early in town for the fall quarter, and rather than watch reruns of Monty Python on a Friday night, I decided to go out. While sipping pissy Coors at a collegiate watering hole called the Graduate, and listening to *My Sharona*—the song that launched Weird Al's career while a DJ at Cal Poly's radio station KCPR FM—a blue-eyed brunette in a corduroy jacket with cool elbow patches walked in. She was with friends, and they all sat down at a nearby table. I walked over, and asked her to dance. Robert Palmer, Bon Jovi and the B-52s boomed from mega speakers mounted above a large, wooden dance floor. We danced, drank beer and talked until closing time.

Her name was Mary Bridget, and she liked Edward Abbey—one of my favorite authors. She was an Applied Art and Design major. When I told her I was studying to be a Park Ranger, her eyes lit up. We started dating, and I quickly learned that Mary B, like me, had an insatiable curiosity for the natural world. We spent most of our time together outdoors, especially at the bird sanctuary in Morro Bay. While walking a trail one day, she came across a large white splattering on the ground.

"Ranger," she asked, "what kind of bird craps like this?"

I came over and studied the ground. It looked like a clumsy painter spilled a gallon of white paint.

"A big bird, probably," I surmised.

"And you call yourself a Ranger?" she said, laughing.

When we weren't hurling eucalyptus seed pods at each other (Mary B was remarkably accurate with her throws), we hiked, and she helped me collect plant specimens to press for my dendrology class.

Following my summer as a fire lookout at Bandelier, I applied for a seasonal National Park Service interpretive position for the summer of 1981. The competition for temporary NPS Park Ranger positions was fierce. Men and women with PhDs after their names competed for GS-4 positions (roughly $5.30/hour). I didn't get so much as a sniff, so enrolled for the summer quarter at Poly. But Bandelier's pull was a reckoning force, and over spring break I convinced Mary B that we should visit. I wanted to show her the fire tower where I had lived and witnessed so many dazzling sunsets, and listen again to the gaseous nighthawks.

We took her Bug, a red 1969 automatic stick shift model, she nicknamed Red Ruby. We grabbed corn nuts at the Cork 'n Bottle, and headed east. While going through the Mojave Desert, Mary B applied cold rags to my neck and back. We made bets about which word we'd see more on the billboards lining the Mother Road. I chose cigs. Mary B chose moccasins. Moccasins won.

We arrived at Frijoles Canyon on a mid-June evening, and drove straight to the fire tower. I was excited about the prospect of standing side-by-side on its balcony with Mary B, the two of us silhouetted by a flaming sunset. The sunset that particular evening however, proved as dull and uninspiring as an algebra problem. In the skies high above the fire tower though, an uninhibited whoopee-cushion sound rang out. A male nighthawk was on the prowl. *Hope you're faring better than me, fella.*

The next morning, we hiked the Frey Trail down to the VC. The sperm counts of the Piñon pines were off the charts. Copious, fine pollen grains coated everything in sight, leaving yellow residues so thick, you could write your name in it.

By the time we arrived at the VC, we were thirsty and covered in saffron-tinted dust. The Chief of Interpretation for Bandelier, a stout Kentuckian named Ed Greene, stood on the front porch of the VC talking with one of his doctoral interpreters. The man sneezed repeatedly, and blew his reddened nose. Pollen was making his life unbearable. He told the Chief his wife and young son were also allergic to the Piñons, so much so, they wore surgical masks whenever they ventured outside. He struggled to hold back histamine-fueled tears, as he told his boss he had to leave. The Chief looked at him and shrugged his shoulders. There wasn't a whole lot he could do. His interpretive lineup was short one. "I'm sorry," he said.

He turned to me and Mary B, who happened to be standing on the portal at the time, and overheard the sad conversation.

"You want a job, Dutton?" he asked, in his distinctive drawl.

I looked at the Chief, surprised.

"Yes, sir," I answered. "When would I start?"

The Chief shot me a sideways look.

"Yesterday."

Talk about being in the right place at the right time!

Life in a Fish Bowl

I love doubleheaders. That way I get to
keep my uniform on longer.
~ Tommy Lasorda

After the Chief offered me the position of NPS seasonal Park Interpreter, I had four days to get my affairs in order and report to duty. Mary B and I hopped into Red Ruby and raced back to San Luis Obispo. I watered my curling Ficus, un-enrolled from summer school, and had a bittersweet farewell dinner with Mary B at our favorite Chinese restaurant—Mee Heng Low. I really didn't want to leave. I wanted to stay and spend my summer with her. But it was an opportunity I couldn't pass up. She helped me pack my old army duffel bag until it looked like the stitching would rip. Then I caught a bumpy, barfy flight to Los Alamos, New Mexico. Along the way, I managed to purchase a pair of over-priced leather shoes that pinched my toes. I buffed them to an NPS cordovan-brown high-gloss.

And so, on my first day as an official National Park Service Ranger at Bandelier National Monument, my feet ached. The rest of my uniform—gray, short sleeve shirt and olive-drab, wool trousers—fit nicely. Creased from crotch to collar, I centered my brand new Smokey the Bear hat in the mirror, and headed out the front door for the VC, chest in the lead.

My quarters throughout the summer of 1981 were a two bedroom, plywood shack, constructed during the Manhattan

Project to house scientists from nearby Los Alamos. I shared my new home with other tenants, none of whom paid a nickel of rent. Field mice scampered across the linoleum floors, or scrimmaged under my bed at night. Bullsnakes waited outside for the mice to leave, but eventually grew impatient and invited themselves in. I would've offered them a beer for their services, except I didn't have enough glasses to go around. Plus, some of the snakes I pulled from under the couch looked underage.

My route to work took me right by the corrals where the Service kept horses for backcountry use. Nakai, a tall, chocolate gelding with bony knees, and a snow white triangle stenciled between brown eyes, waltzed over, looking for a handout. I soon discovered that sure-footed Nakai munched on anything within reach—fence posts, cactus, juniper trees, yucca plants...Ranger hats. On this morning, he walked his fuzzy lips over some sugar cubes I had in my outstretched palm.

During my walk to the VC, I paused by the shimmering El Rito de Los Frijoles, the river that sustained life for the Anasazi people who inhabited Bandelier two thousand years earlier. Three miles down canyon, it merged with the mighty Rio Grande—a 1,900 mile long waterway that stretched from south-central Colorado to the Gulf of Mexico.

In the understory, orange and black Rufous-sided towhees scratched in thick pine duff, looking for grubs. Turkey vultures flapped like winged drunks in the cloudless sky overhead. One of them spiraled out of the sky and awkwardly hopped over to a mangled, greasy lump of fur on the road. After snatching some glistening entrails, pillorying the carcass with its hooked bill, other buzzards flew down and helped themselves to the all-you-can-eat roadkill smorgasbord. "Finders, keepers," is not an axiom shared by scavengers.

Whiptail lizards, with their loud racing stripes and long tails, also scrimmaged in the leaf litter next to the towhees. They reminded me of NASCAR drivers, especially when they darted into Bandelier's two-lane entrance road, eluding passing cars. On this morning, one lizard seemed inordinately suicidal.

"Hey, Ranger, can I turn around down there?"

I turned to see a man sitting in a dually truck, pulling a fifth wheel. A round woman sat next him, and a small boy in the backseat pressed his face to the glass. At that moment, a bulgy-eyed whiptail raced out between the truck's axles.

"Yes sir, you can."

"Thanks," he said, inching forward, narrowly missing the Richard Petty of whiptails.

Questions. Park Rangers across the land get asked them everyday. It's part of the job. In the grocery store—what aisle are the pickled olives on? In the Nation's capital—can I park my car on Constitution Avenue? At the airport—has that United flight been canceled? At the big box store—how many miles can I get on these radials? Standing in line at the precinct—do I have the right ballot? Wearing a uniform in public, I found out, practically makes you an authority on damn near everything.

Two tour buses parked outside the VC had beaten me to work. As they spewed noxious diesel, Kristen, my supervisor, came running out of the VC, Stetson in hand. Her tiny cordovan brown shoes scuffed on the flagstone as she hurried along. Long brown hair trailed behind her. Unlike my own, her shoes were considerably more worn.

"Dave, would you please talk to this Japanese tour group? I have a ruins walk in five minutes. They just sort of showed up."

"No problem."

"Thanks, Dave."

Kristen was wed to the NPS, and was Bandelier's fiercest warrior. During my previous summer as an SCA, I once saw her chastise a burly Texan. "Please stay on the trail," she'd instructed him, in a tone a mother would use when telling her child to "not touch."

As Kristen retreated back into the VC, a diminutive Japanese man stepped off the tour bus, shouting orders. He wore a New York Yankees ball cap that rested on his ears. He shouted at me. "We see park now! We have 45 minutes!"

Mister, that isn't enough time to scratch your butt and get a Coke! Bandelier offered some of the finest examples of prehistoric

Indian dwellings in the American Southwest. Allotting less than an hour to see them, didn't seem right. Unfortunately, arbitrary time constraints were an irritating reality of a Park Ranger's job. People were always in a hurry, foregoing a longer stay in order to see something else on their hectic itinerary.

The tour director pointed to his watch again, then darted back onto the buses, yelling orders like a drill sergeant. The occupants tumbled out into a bright New Mexico sun. I was surrounded by middle-aged Japanese women carrying Gucci purses, sporting acid-wash jeans and penny loafers. One woman, whose head barely came to my chest, grabbed my arm and smiled as she posed for a picture. Asahflex, Nikon and Yashica SLR's clicked furiously, as everyone took turns posing with the Park Ranger in the big hat.

"We love Smokey Bear," they said, pointing at my hat. I smiled proudly, and motioned for the group to move in closer. Using my best Park Ranger voice, I began…

"Welcome to Band—"

From the back of the crowd, the tour director began shouting in Japanese again. In unison, his flock turned and advanced on the VC, leaving me and the stinking buses in their wake. I watched as they bottlenecked at the VC doors, before breaking through and mobbing the small sales counter in the corner of the VC.

I threaded my way through the group, and took a position behind the information desk. Over the din of foreign voices, I heard a familiar one—Mrs. Frey. She toiled behind a cash register, trying to keep up with the sudden onslaught. Stacked three deep, the Japanese shelled out greenbacks, buying Native American CD's, postcards, books and posters. The cash register chimed like a Vegas slot machine.

"David, can you help me?" Mrs. Frey pleaded.

"I'll be right over."

I made my way to the sales desk, and looked at the green LED display on the cash register.

"Mrs. Frey," I said, "you have a $6,000,000 dollar overring."

"Oh dear, I seem to have charged someone too much!" she said, putting a small hand over her mouth.

"Yes, ma'am."

We shared a good laugh. We always did. I silenced the squeal coming from the register, while Mrs. Frey rang up purchases, being careful not to add any more zeroes.

"Which way is Tewahnee?" the Japanese tour director asked. He was referring to *Tyuonyi* (chew-OHN-yee), the main Anasazi ruin in Frijoles canyon. I pointed him in the right direction, and the tour shuffled through the backdoors of the VC, carrying their purchases in plastic Southwest Parks and Monuments bags.

As they exited, a young black couple entered the VC. They smiled at me and Mrs. Frey then turned their attention to a corn exhibit next to the front door. Mrs. Frey's hearing aid began to squeal, which it often did. The louder it squealed, the louder she spoke. She began to talk about Negroes.

"You know, David," she said dramatically, as if delivering a Shakespearean soliloquy... *God, Mrs. Frey, not NOW...* "I think in the Deep South they call them niggers."

Mrs. Frey's hearing aid trumpeted, and she spoke louder.

"We don't see many black people in New Mexico, David," she shouted.

The couple wheeled around and glared full-on at me. After all, I was in uniform, not Mrs. Frey. As far as I knew she hadn't a prejudiced molecule in her body. But none of that mattered. At that moment, I just wished I was someplace else. My face blistered. I wanted to say something, but didn't. I just stood there, embarrassed.

After an interminable silence, the couple exited the VC, just as the family in the truck I'd met on my walk to work entered it. With hands clasped behind their backs, they studied a clay replica of Tyuonyi, mounted under glass in the center of the VC. The man and the boy wore creased blue jeans and identical Alamo T-shirts. In the man's back pocket was a Skoal can. The woman teetered on high heels. She wore purple shorts, which tested the tensile strength of the fabric. Her white tank top had a blotched, red stain, probably escaped chile from a breakfast burrito.

"Sir, is this what the Indians lived in?" she asked. Her accent was thicker than country gravy.

"Yes ma'am. That is how it may have looked 500 years ago."

Then I asked her if they were going to visit the ruins. She looked up from the exhibit, annoyed.

"No sir," she pointedly answered. "We're from Texas!"

What the f---?

It completely took me off-guard. It was as if what she said was an incontrovertible fact. And to her, it probably was. Like, "the best part of waking up is Folgers in your cup" or "blondes have more fun." I pictured a Texas visitor's guide—the kind you get at an interstate Welcome Center along with teeny cups of shitty coffee—with the words "No Sir, We're From Texas!" emblazoned on the cover. I looked at her, dumfounded.

"Oh," was the best I could manage.

Kristen returned from her Ruins Walk—the one she was scheduled to do when the Japanese tour group showed up. Her cheeks were flushed, courtesy of a June New Mexico sun.

"Dave, there are lots of people in the canyon this morning. I'd like for you to do some roving interpretation."

"You bet."

After the morning I was having, I was eager to escape the VC. I grabbed my Ranger hat and walkie-talkie, waved bye to Mrs. Frey, and headed for the back door. Roving interpretation allowed for one-on-one contact with the public, or as "The trail to FRIJOLES Ruins" booklet described it, "The uniformed employees of the National Park Service are here to serve you, and welcome the opportunity to make your stay more enjoyable." I set a course for Ceremonial Cave, a mile upstream of the VC. There'd be fewer people along that route. My path took me along the meandering Frijoles creek, where I spied a wayward whiptail lizard sitting catawampus on a rock. Where a long, sleek tail should have been, there was just a bulbous stub.

Lizards are the undeniable sorcerers of the reptilian world. In addition to spurting blood from sinuses above their eyes to confuse predators (as some horned lizards can do), they have even a niftier trick—voluntarily loosing their tails. When in danger of becoming a meal, lizards can detach their tails, leaving them writhing on the ground like unattended fire hoses. Predators attuned to movement pounce on the squirming tails, allowing for escape. Although losing an appendage seems draconian, it's a very effective strategy. The predator gets the tail, but the lizard lives for another day. Many whiptail lizard species are asexual (they don't require males to produce offspring), so only female heirs are produced. The chances of this lizard recounting her harrowing getaway during an all-girl whiptail slumber party were pretty good.

The radio on my hip crackled to life. It was VC dispatch. "We have an incident in the main canyon and assistance is needed."

I keyed my mike. "I'm close by," I radioed.

I turned around and headed for Tyuonyi. When I got to the main canyon ruin, visitors had jammed up near the cliff trail where it narrowed between two thick tuff monoliths along a south facing wall. I hiked to a higher point and looked down. I heard a woman's voice. It sounded like the lady from Texas I'd met in the VC earlier in the morning. Somehow, she'd managed to wedge herself between two rock slabs, and was impossibly stuck. I worked my way down to her. A man's voice coming from the other side of the woman said "Push."

It was Ranger Sam, my roommate, and unquestionably the hairiest man on the planet. Sam had floor mats for hair. He made Sean Connery look like a naked mole rat. Whenever Sam shaved, he started at his collarbone.

Unlike me, Sam was a law enforcement Park Ranger. We were about the same age. He grew up in New York, and was Italian—the kind that could have you fitted with concrete shoes and tossed into the Hudson River. Or so he said. I figured he was bullshitting—until he glared at me one day with his thick, black unibrow. Then, I felt I could be disappeared.

One afternoon during a monsoon downpour, Sam and I were drinking cold Oly's under the carport. He told me that he worked at the Statue of Liberty. I loved his stories about Rangering there, because I hadn't a clue as to what East Coast Park Rangers dealt with. Sam eventually grew tired of the Statue, and figured a change in scenery would do him some good, so he packed his bags and headed 2,000 miles west. I think Sam really preferred the hustle and jive of throngs of people, and not necessarily an unostentatious western park. I found Bandelier's stillness comforting. It was one of the reasons I enjoyed working there. Tranquility though, was driving Sam batshit.

As a law enforcement Ranger, Sam needed to drive a patrol vehicle. One afternoon, while returning from White Rock, I fell in behind Sam, who was taking his driving test. The Chief Law Enforcement Ranger sat in the passenger seat next to him. Sam struggled to keep the government truck on his side of the double yellow line, as he negotiated a curvy stretch of road. Red brake lights flashed, as the truck spasmed and jerked. At the last possible moment, the Chief reached over and yanked the steering wheel like a panicked driving school instructor, keeping it from careening over the mesa.

By late summer, Sam was up to his bushy eyebrows in sereneness. He packed up and headed east, presumably back to the hubbub and hullabaloo of Mother Liberty. I would miss our carport scuttlebutt sessions.

"Push," Sam said, "again."

"I'm trying," I said, straining.

It was awkward. I wasn't sure where to properly put my hands. I was in uncharted territory. The woman's largesse filled the void between the rock slabs like air in a tire. I regrouped and decided to push on her hips, and found my hands slowly disappearing into the purple fabric of her shorts.

"Push harder!" Sam shouted.

I changed hand positions and pushed straight into the back of her bulgy tank top. I sensed a shift. Sam did too, and with one last heave, she popped free from her rock vice like a cork from a champagne bottle. She fell onto one knee, crying. Her husband rushed over and lifted her up. *That's one strong Texan!* Her little boy was crying. I felt profoundly sorry for her. This certainly wasn't the National Park memory they'd hoped for.

Sam tended to the woman and I directed foot traffic until a call came over the radio requesting his assistance at the Juniper Campground up on the mesa. The woman and her family slowly headed down the trail. It was almost noon, so I headed for the curio shop for lunch. I smelled Sally Fries—a myocardial concoction of grilled French fries and green chile, smothered in cheese. I collected my order, and walked out to the concession patio. In the VC parking lot, a car engine shrieked. Blue exhaust wafted over the lunch crowd like fog.

Everyone looked up from their Frito pies and green chile cheeseburgers. In the words of a future boss, they looked disgruntled (*adj.* to put into a state of sulky dissatisfaction). No vote was taken, but I seemed to be their unanimous choice to deal with the calamity. I put Sally and my Coke down, and walked out to the parking lot to investigate.

Mrs. Frey sat in her shaking Dodge Rambler, blissfully unaware that the car looked ready to jettison at any moment. Exhaust spewed from the tailpipe, swirling up cyclonic clouds of dust and pine needles. I walked around to the passenger side, and knocked on the window. Mrs. Frey rolled it down and began speaking. Her rosy lips moved, but the fully-throttled engine drowned out her words. She had the gas pedal pressed to the floorboard.

"Mrs. Frey," I shouted, "let off the gas!"

I wasn't sure her hearing aid was on, but she released the accelerator. The Rambler sputtered briefly, then resumed a normal pulse.

"Hello, David," she said. A lingering exhaust cloud puffed past us.

"Mrs. Frey, what's wrong with your car?"

"The nice man at the gas station said my battery was low."

She went on to explain that the mechanic advised her to race the engine to recharge her battery. He probably figured she'd drive the car to charge it up, but Mrs. Frey, being almost ninety, understood things differently. I convinced her she could idle the engine for twenty minutes, and charge the battery that way. Her eyes twinkled, and she put a downy-soft hand on mine.

"David," she said, "I'll buy you an ice cream the next time we go into White Rock."

I often chauffeured Mrs. Frey to town on my days off so she could grocery shop. I was twenty-five years old, an army veteran, had slept with women, but in Mrs. Frey's eyes, I was still in Sunday school.

"Yes ma'am, I'll look forward to it," I said, then walked back to the Curio shop.

At 2:00, I sat in the headquarters lobby with my feet up, enjoying the air conditioning. I was scheduled to conduct a children's program at 2:30. *Maybe we won't have any takers this afternoon?* Kristen burst through the front door. We had takers.

I walked across the hot parking lot to the VC. A little boy and his mom stood in the shade under the portal. He was a cute kid with moppy hair, maybe six or seven. Then again, he could've been ten. I'm terrible at guessing kid's ages. I took a knee and introduced myself, extending a hand. The boy looked up at his mother. She nodded her approval, and he put his tiny hand in mine. We shook. We had a pact.

"Well then, you ready to go?" I asked.

The boy looked up at me, waved goodbye to his mom, and we set a course for Frijoles creek. A cool creek on a scorching afternoon...*how can you go wrong?*

As we walked, the boy wrapped his small fingers around my own. He looked up at me with smiling eyes, like I was his dad or big brother. I suddenly felt protective, and wondered if he had a father to take him fishing or a big brother to shoot hoops with. We found a shady pool along Frijoles Creek, peeled off our shoes and socks, rolled up our pant legs, and waded in. Clear, mountain water washed over our toes—his, small and white, mine large and gnarly.

For the next hour, we splashed in the creek, turning over rocks and plucking prehistoric looking damselfly exoskeletons from underneath them. We chased a small Brook trout, but with one flick of its golden caudal fin, the fish torpedoed upstream into the shadows. We marveled at glittering electric-blue colored minerals in the sandy creek bottom, and almost caught an unsuspecting garter snake lying on the bank. But like the Brook trout, the snake whipped its slender body and vanished into some reeds.

When it was time to head back to the VC, I sat on the bank and tied my tortuous shoes, which had long since lost their shiny cordovan luster. A shadow arched across my peripheral and landed in front of me, making a loud ka-plunk! A tsunami of cold creek water washed over me. I looked up. On the opposite bank, a barefoot boy stood grinning from ear to ear. Ripples backhanded the bank. The humongous rock he'd hosed me with lay embedded in the sandy creek bottom. *Damn thing is half his weight. Good job kid!*

The boy's mother was waiting for us when we got back to the VC. She eyed our soggy appearance.

"We almost caught a snake mom! And there were all these cool looking blue things in the sand."

The boy's mother smiled. You could tell she knew her son had a good time. She thanked me, then gently grabbed her son's hand, and headed for the Curio shop. The boy looked back over his shoulder, and waved goodbye. I waved back. The summer dad took us to the Grand Tetons, a Park Ranger bent a knee and listened patiently as I recounted my harrowing tale of eluding thuggish bears one cold night. *I'm just paying it forward, kid.*

For the last hour of my first day, I dried out behind the information desk. Kristen stopped by. She told me some disturbing things about the little boy I'd just spent an hour in the woods with. He'd been sexually abused by his stepfather, and was frightened of men. In fact, his mother had serious misgivings about allowing her baby boy on a hike alone with a male Ranger. Only after Kristen convinced the woman that it would be okay, did she relent.

"Anyway," Kristen said, eying my wet shirt, "looks like you two kids had a good time."

As I walked past the stables on my way home late in the afternoon, Nakai strutted over looking for a handout. I rubbed his furry ears and whispered I'd have something for him tomorrow. He gave me a discerning look and walked away, swishing flies with his long, wiry tail.

"Hey," I called out, "if you can't trust a Ranger, who can you trust?"

I continued up the road to my plywood Ritz. Sam sat under the carport, a tall Oly in hand.

"Hey Ranger," he shouted, "did you hear about the lady that got stuck in the ruins today?"

Walk a Mile in a Man's Shoes

There is this to be said for walking: It's the one mode
of human locomotion by which a man proceeds on
his own two feet, upright, erect, as a man should be,
not squatting on his rear haunches like a frog.
~ Edward Abbey

The clock on the kitchen wall read 7:49 am. I had eleven minutes to make a sandwich, lace up my boots, and get to the VC. Today, I would lead a nature walk to the Lower Falls of Frijoles Canyon. I navigated threadbare laces through a maze of boot grommets, cinching them tight. Snap! A frayed boot string dangled in my palm. Looking down, I counted five bulgy knots. Traversing Bandelier's backcountry—a world only the hardiest park visitors ever experienced—was taking its toll on my boots, and my feet!

I melded the broken laces with my sixth square knot, walked to the kitchen, and peered into the refrigerator: dated carton of chocolate milk, near empty jar of grape jelly, a sprouting onion, a half loaf of Wonder Bread, and a lone can of Olympia beer. *How's a guy supposed to make it on a Ranger's salary when Oly sets you back $1.50?*

It was the summer of 1982—a tough time to be a government employee. President Reagan was in office. It's never reassuring to government employees when the Chief declares publicly, "Government is the problem." Seasonal Park Ranger jobs were scarce. Permanent Park Ranger positions—the ones with benefits—scarcer still. I reached for the twins, Smuckers and Jiffy, feeling lucky to have a *goberhment* job at all.

I wrapped my thick-as-a-brick P&J in wax paper and stuffed it into my backpack, along with a pulpy apple, water bottle, extra socks, bird identification book, binoculars, and first aid kit. I grabbed my NPS radio and rushed out the front door.

When I got to the VC, a young couple stood around a wall mounted map of the monument. The young woman had braided blond hair, tight shorts, and a knapsack slung over her shoulder. Her milky white legs were toned. The man was stocky and also wore shorts. Both wore sandals. *Must be European.*

The woman saw me approaching, and spoke first. "Vere ist dis place the fahls ya?"

Yep.

I introduced myself, extending a hand. She shook it firmly. Her eyes were bluer than a summer New Mexico sky.

"My name ist Claudia." She pronounced it *klow-dia*. "Unt, dis ist Dieter. Vee are from Switzerland. It's our voneymoon."

"Ello," said Dieter.

I looked down at Claudia's candy apple red toenails.

"The falls trail is kind of rugged," I said. "I'm not sure sandals are a good idea."

During two summers at Bandelier, I'd hiked many miles of the monument's backcountry. I knew firsthand what sharp basalt could do, even to a foot ensconced in a sturdy hiking boot. Claudia shot me a don't-be-silly look.

"In Switzerland people valk," she explained. "Ve hike everyvhere."

Well, that ends that. In Switzerland they valk!

"Okay then, let's go."

We began walking towards the trailhead to the Lower Falls when Claudia stopped suddenly, and knelt down. A shiny black beetle clumsily advanced in her direction. The insect stopped at her red toes, and raised its abdomen straight into the air—the insect equivalent of "the finger." Fortunately for my Swiss lovers, their guide had almost passed his Cal Poly Entomology class. I recognized the creature as a stink beetle, and launched into a dissertation about the characteristics of the order Coleoptera, the one to which beetles belong.

"There are over 350,000 species of beetles in the world," I began. "In fact, beetles account for about a quarter of all life forms on the planet."

It was pretty clear that Claudia and Dieter were not impressed with my factoids. They both studied the insect, which still had its ass pointed up at them.

"Beetles also have unique wing structures," I continued, "the hind wings being more membranous than the front, which serve as protective sheaths."

"Vhy is dis butt in se air?" Claudia asked, cupping the cute little beetle in her palm.

"No, don't pick it—"

Kayakers on the Rio Grande miles downstream heard Claudia's shrieks. Stink beetles, if provoked, spew foul smelling liquid from their abdomens. Claudia's specimen was an emitter of the highest order, the potentate of stink. She tossed the beetle, watching it fall the human equivalent of 30 stories. The creature righted itself, and continued on its way, unharmed. Claudia sniffed her palm, and recoiled in disgust. She turned to her hubby, but he backed away. In the game of stink tag, Claudia was *it*.

We'd just started down the falls trail, when I began to get a feeling that something was watching us. Except for the babbling El Rito de Los Frijoles below, the canyon was uncharacteristically still—no chirping birds, no scurrying whiptails, no rustling pine boughs, nothing. Then, I heard droning, like a distant swarm of bees. It seemed to be coming from some waist-high chamisa bushes, just off the trail. I approached, slowly. The droning grew more intense. In the thick dust, I saw tracks leading to the bushes. Something heavy had been dragged this way. *But what?* Feeling like a rookie homicide detective at a crime scene, I stooped and parted the chamisa.

Scores of metallic Bottle flies jostled and collided above the glistening entrails of a mule deer buck, vying for the juiciest spots to deposit their egg payloads. The monument had 32,000 acres of wilderness, yet these flies knew exactly where to be and when. Blood spilled over the buck's eviscerated abdominal cavity, forming crimson pools in the powdery, rhyolitic dirt. The hairs on the back of my neck stiffened. *This is a fresh mountain lion kill.*

I stood and looked around. The cat was likely still close, watching. Mountain lions have more aliases than a porn star—cougar, catamount, panther, puma—all of which belie its Latin name, *Felis concolor*, meaning cat of the same color. *I don't care what damn color the cat is, I'm getting the hell out of here!* I turned and hurriedly returned to the trail.

"Vhat vas dat?" Claudia asked. She had a worried look on her face.

"A mountain lion kill," I answered. "The lion might still be close by. We should keep going."

For the next hour, we walked in silence, descending deeper into Frijoles Canyon, kicking up ankle-high plumes of dust as we went. It was hot and bone dry. The monsoon rains were a month away. Suddenly, I heard Dieter shouting behind me. In a thick European accent, it sounded like he was saying *ass*. I turned and saw Dieter making exaggerated circular motions with his arm, like a third base coach waving in the winning run. He pointed to a clump of weeds a yard or two off the trail.

What the…?

An image unfolded in my head. I was a Jeopardy contestant, dressed in an ill-fitting suit and crooked tie, manically thumbing the buzzer.

"I'll take Herpetology for 300, Alex."

"First described by Linnaeus in 1758, this species' Latin name means 'shield.'"

"What is the Asp Viper?"

"Yes, you are correct."

"Herpetology for 400…"

From my herpetology class at Poly, I recalled a species of poisonous snake which inhabits the Swiss Alps, known as the Asp viper. Might my *voneymooners* be confusing an Asp for a rattlesnake? *Only one way to find out.*

I left the trail and approached the weed patch Dieter pointed at. I could make out a snake, thick as a Michelob bottle. The serpent had beautiful cream and diagonal brown markings across its broad back. *A Diamondback rattler?* I worked my way upslope, keeping a watchful eye on the snake's massive head. Its tail lashed at the dry grass under scale, creating a menacing buzz. The snake reared up and contorted into an "S" shape, preparing to strike.

"Vatch out Mr. Dutton!" Claudia shouted. "The ass vill bite you."

Now, I was close enough to see the snake's tail. What I didn't see is what herpetologists refer to as "buttons" or rattles—interlocking chambers made from keratin, the same material as human fingernails. When vibrated, they make a distinctive rattle. This snake however, was buttonless, and doing its scaly best to convince me it was a fearsome Western Diamondback rattlesnake, except it wasn't. It was a nonpoisonous Bullsnake—the biggest I'd ever seen. I reached down and grabbed the charlatan's tail, just as it bolted for the cover of a Prickly pair cactus.

The snake was as long as an NBA forward is tall. I could feel his cool skin squeezing my bicep and forearm. His belly scales, or "scutes," were iridescent. He'd recently shed his old skin—the reptilian equivalent of a factory paint job.

"It's a Bullsnake," I shouted triumphantly to Claudia and Dieter, who were backpedaling down the trail. "It's not poisonous."

Claudia approached first. Dieter however, had no interest in the Asp. When she got within touching range Claudia asked, "Vill it bite me?"

"Nope," I said, "only Texans."

She moved an elegant finger along the snake's back. "The skin ist cool, ya?"

She flashed me a girlish grin. I smiled back so hard my mustache stood straight out from my upper lip.

"Would you like to hold the snake?" I asked.

To my surprise, she did. The snake repositioned itself on her nape, taking in the view from on high.

"Vat ist doing?"

"He's sunning himself. He looks very content."

Claudia gestured for Dieter to come over and see the snake on her back, but Dieter wasn't having any of it. He clearly wasn't comfortable with his new bride, Medusa.

After a few minutes, I pulled the snake off Claudia's white shoulders and released it next to the trail. It spiraled around a low-hanging juniper branch like an Olympic gymnast on the uneven bars. Then, the three of us resumed our hike. Dieter shuffled last, head down—our group's Eeyore.

Soon, we reached a point in the trail that afforded a panoramic view of the Upper Falls of Frijoles Canyon. The sun was in full splendor, heating the canyon walls, creating updrafts. Turkey vultures spiraled erratically on the thermals, as if at any moment, they'd crash out of the sky. Pugnacious Canyon wrens, with their descending *tee-tee-tee-tee* notes, flitted about the rocks. Low lying Cholla cacti clung stubbornly to vertical cliff faces.

In this area of Frijoles Canyon, dark basalt rock contrasts sharply with lighter volcanic ash above it, giving the appearance of a layered cake. Over millennia, the waters of Frijoles Creek had knifed through the soft volcanic tuff. The juxtaposition of the two rock strata—one soft and one hard—created the Upper Falls. The little rito, no longer shackled by banks, hurled itself over the canyon lip, plummeting eighty feet to clear pools below.

We paused, taking in the extraordinary view, then negotiated spiraling switchbacks down to the verdant oasis of Frijoles Creek below us. Crossing a wooden footbridge, we stopped for lunch under a shady Cottonwood. I rummaged through my dusty backpack, looking for my water bottle. Claudia and Dieter played footsy in a small eddy. Her bright red toenails looked like brilliant red rubies in the clear water. Dieter seemed to have forgiven his bride for her snake handling. They laughed and splashed and carried on. I felt like a pimply teenager at prom—the kid with the mustard tuxedo and no date.

After lunch, we pushed on to the Rio Grande. By this point, we'd descended 700 feet into a landscape unlike any other in the monument. Sparsely vegetated and barren, the latte-colored Rio Grande seemed to be the only thing in this part of the monument with a pulse. While Claudia and Dieter walked the muddy banks of the river, I found a Ponderosa log, which long ago decided to fall over, and took off my boot. A gnawing pain in my little toe needed tending to.

"Vhat ist dat?" Claudia called out.

Shit, again?

I slid my sock and boot back on, and limped down to the Rio. Across the river, two emaciated cows nibbled on some Cholla cacti. They looked like four-legged skeletons draped in threadbare carpets.

"They're cows," I said.

"Cows?" Dieter asked. It sounded like *cauls.*

"Yes."

"But vhat do they eat?" Claudia asked.

"Sometimes they'll eat cactus," I said.

The reality was that grazing cattle didn't belong in a congressionally designated wilderness. A debate called the "Sagebrush Rebellion," raged in the arid West, which pitted environmental groups against ranching and mining interests. The Sagebrush rebels wanted the federal government to relinquish more control of vast western lands to state and local authorities. Ostensibly, this would speed the growth of emerging western economies. They reasoned that although sagebrush lacked aesthetic qualities, public lands could be useful for grazing, off-road vehicles, or even something environmentally friendly, like mining. I did not share their view. To me, public land is public land. It belongs to all of us. And it doesn't make a wit of difference if you never set foot in Bandelier's backcountry. At least you can go to sleep knowing *it* is there, and that it is being protected. Not only was I all in for the protectionists, I was growing damned tired of stepping in cow shit during my walkabouts in the monument.

"But there's no grass for sem to eat," Dieter said.

"In Switzerland, cauls are fat," Claudia chimed in.

I pictured absurdly wide cows with immense udders, swishing their tails and chewing their cud, while in the background, lush green hills loomed large, like those in *The Sound of Music*. The gaunt creatures by the Rio Grande could only dream of such a grassy Mecca, and judging from their skeletal outlines, they hadn't long to do that.

I limped back to my pine tree, and tended to my sore toe. To the west, thunder boomed. Dark, anvil-topped clouds were forming, and the air became noticeably more humid. Between thunder vibes, I heard Claudia's soft voice, beckoning.

"You should come in Vanger Dutton, the vater ist fine, ya."

The moleskin would have to wait. I laced up again and walked down to the river. Two impossibly white bodies frolicked in the coffee-colored river. Claudia was naked! I assumed Dieter was too, but didn't care. Their clothes were strewn over a dead juniper tree along the bank.

Claudia was waist deep in the river. Her wet blonde hair hung low across her chest, giving cover to her small breasts. I stood on the bank, in my sweaty NPS uniform and dusty boots, staring at Claudia, not quite sure what to do. Claudia flashed a smile. *Hoping I take you up on your offer?* Dieter swam over to his glistening bride, and wrapped his muscular arms around her. He shot me a look: Go find your own vermaid, Vanger!

Claudia repeated her invite. "You should come in Vanger Dutton."

"I really shouldn't."

"Vhy?"

Vhy? At that very moment, I could've stripped down and cannonballed off the bank. But I was a National Park Service Ranger, and, well...*There needs to be some decorum, damnit!* An ear-splitting thunderclap heralded the advance of an approaching storm, giving me a desperately needed out.

"Looks like a storm is coming. We probably should head back."

Claudia frowned and climbed out of the river first, followed by Dieter. I looked the other way, but not before he reached for his lederhosen. Dieter was hung!

I limped back to my Ponderosa refuge for the third time. As I attended to my plum-colored little toe, my mind drifted back to something that happened a few weeks earlier, not far from where I now laced up my boots.

It was midweek, and I'd decided to hike to the Rio Grande on my day off. No one would be there. The place would be all mine, just like a Club Med beach, only with rattlesnakes, biting flies and prickly pear cacti. When I reached the river, it was bank-full with alpine snowmelt. Feeling decidedly free, I took off my clothes and swam out to a sand bar in the middle of the river. The water was frigid, and the current much swifter than I thought. I struggled to get to the island. When I got there, I turned over, exhausted. The warming rays of a mid-June sun felt good. It was the perfect juxtaposition—coolness below, warmth above. Lying naked on the sandbar, I listened to the rushing water of the Rio, and closer in, ripples kissing the island's edge. Then I heard girl's voices.

I flipped over. On the opposite bank, weaving through one story high Tamarisk, were dozens of young girls, shouldering colorful backpacks, laughing as they went. *Girl Scouts?* I scurried sideways like a crab at the beach, and sought cover behind a dilapidated Ponderosa that had beached itself during spring runoff. Immediately, black ants emerged from the tree. Ants are social insects, and in their communicative secretions, I'm sure there was a coded message: Hey everyone, come see the naked giant! Hordes of ants scurried out from their log sanctum to see what all the commotion was about.

I slapped away ants with one hand. With the other, I covered my groin. I peeked over the Ponderosa. The girls idled about, sipping from water bottles, and eating from bright foil wrappers. The ants, however, were not so idle. They covered my body like a black hairnet.

After what seemed like an eternity (but was probably only minutes) I looked again. The girls had finished their lunch and were mounting up. When I looked again, they were slowly making their way up Frijoles Canyon. I couldn't wait any longer. I plunged into the Rio, taking swarms of ants with me, and began swimming. The current carried me yards downstream from where my clothes were piled. I walked back along the bank shivering, pulled on my clothes, and flicked one last adventurous ant from my ear. *Club Med my ass.*

#

"Vee are ready to go, ya."

Claudia's warm voice melted my icy Rio Grande memory. She stood over me. Her wet blonde locks hung down like straggly ropes.

I stuffed my foot into my boot and winced. Claudia and Dieter however, showed no ill effects from hiking in sandals. *In Switzerland, people valk.* Dark, moisture-laden clouds began to obscure the late afternoon sun. A take-no-prisoners storm was fast approaching. The three of us set out for the VC; a monstrous thunder clap being our starting pistol.

Soon, we crossed over the wooden footbridge where Claudia and Dieter played footsie. Fecund raindrops pinged off the crowns of Box Elder and Cottonwood trees. We pushed on past the falls, past the spot where Claudia played snake handler with the ass, past the slaughtered buck crime scene. Now though, the fear of seeing a mountain lion was no match for the panic we felt every time lightning zinged above our heads like tracer rounds. A hard falling rain bulleted up dust on the trail, and stung our cheeks. We sprinted the last hundred yards to the VC through a slashing torrent, and reached the parking lot where our journey had been christened by a smelly beetle.

The three of us stood under the VC portal as the storm vented. Sheets of rain washed over the parking lot. Stroboscopic lightning seared the sky in concert with clangorous thunder. Everywhere, people scrambled for cover; the slower and unluckier ones looking like typhoon victims. Rain cascaded from roof *canales* onto the pavement below. Suddenly, Claudia turned and gave me a big, wet hug. Her lithe body was warm. *She smells like the Rio.*

"Vell, Mr. Dutton, thank you for se tour. It vas vonderful."

She smiled at me. I just stood there—a horny, soaked to the bone, Park Ranger.

"You're welcome," was the best could muster.

Claudia and Dieter turned and dashed into the flood, hand-in-hand, waving goodbye as they sloshed to their rental car. Above the roar of pelting rain, Claudia's sweet, accented voice echoed in my mind—"It vas vonderful."

I pulled my NPS ball cap down, and stepped into the monsoon, smiling.

Tomorrow was payday, and Oly was on sale.

Goin' Back to Cali

"California is where you can't run any
further without getting wet."
~ Neil Morgan

In October of 1982, I arrived back at Bandelier National Monument. Armed with a degree in Natural Resources Management from Cal Poly (*oh, you're one of them*), the NPS hired me as a winter seasonal, interpretive Park Ranger. But I didn't show up alone. I had a partner—Mary B. We'd married the month before in a little church in Carmel, California. Two years after Mrs. Frey sent me home with the Hopi good luck ring, and told me I'd meet someone special, Mary B placed a wedding band on my left hand, and I said, "I do." *The Lady of the Canyon damn sure could read a palm!*

We moved into a one-room lodge in Frijoles Canyon, a stones throw from the VC. I'd walk home for lunch, smelling Mary B's sumptuous soups and hearty stews wafting in the canyon air. The edges of my body grew ever rounder.

After dinner, we'd sit out on our portal, glasses of Monterey Riesling in hand, enjoying the Indian summer. Sometimes, we ambled down to the Rito de Los Frijoles and watched as deer tiptoed in on silent hooves, reclaiming their rightful niche. Birds, squirrels and snakes followed suit. Absent the hubbub and mufflers of the day's throngs, the canyon was a much different place. We were lucky to be a part of it.

One evening, after I'd had one glass of vino too many, we strolled down to the river, as we customarily did. A pair of roosting Turkey vultures perched high in a cottonwood tree, peered down at us. When they saw me, they shifted nervously on their branch, like they were on a hot skillet. The calcimine excrement below their roost smelled horrendous. For no apparent reason—other than having too much ethanol in my system—I grabbed a rock and hurled it upward at the birds. The rock arced pitifully short.

"What are you doing Ranger?" Mary B scolded. "You're not supposed to harass the wildlife."

She was right. She almost always was. The park's wildlife was sacrosanct. *I'm going to the dark side.* I capitulated briefly, then chose another, smaller rock, and let it fly. The buzzards craned their red leathery heads and stared down crooked beaks at the besotted Park Ranger sixty feet below.

Fermentation was in full bore, and I was feeling no pain. Tomorrow, I'd probably have to see about Tommy John surgery. But that could wait. I zinged another round. The vultures shifted again. They were in my crosshairs, and they knew it. Something had to be done. I bent down and picked up another rock. Just as I cocked my arm to throw it, the vultures lifted their tails and let loose a pungent volley of mucous, which splashed down like white rain. The stinky, viscous cascade sent me running wildly, arms flailing over my head. Mary B laughed. "See, I told you."

Vultures 1, Ranger 0.

…And that was the end of the great Turkey vulture shootout.

#

During Indian summer nights—like what Bandelier was experiencing in the early fall of 1982—I'd lay awake, wondering what the ancient Anasazi did on nights like this. Did they lay awake too, on their rooftops or in the plaza of *Tyuonyi*, stargazing? Did they tell stories around dying embers? Make love? I convinced myself that a nighttime visit to the ruins was in order. *It might even be romantic.* Thus, on a harvest moon evening, Mary B and I ventured into the ruins. We were, as Cat Stevens coined it, "being followed by a moon shadow." A warm breeze bullied the crowns of pines, sparking choruses of whispers through their boughs. Nothing escaped the moonbeam. Everything from minuscule to magnificent, cast an umbra.

We walked, hand in hand, along the asphalt trail leading west from the back porch of the VC. I'd walked the path hundreds of times while leading tours, but now, bathed in moonlight, the trail looked eerily sinuous. We came to the edge of a roofless, subterranean kiva that the Anasazi once used for ceremonies. Moonlight flooded the kiva like a lunar swimming pool. On the floor of the kiva, in the center, was a small hole known as a sipapu. The Anasazi believed the spirits emerged from the underworld through this tiny portal. Standing at the edge of the kiva, it felt like the spirits were emerging from it now, even if I couldn't see them. I sensed Mary B did too. My idea of a romantic moonlit stroll through the remnants of an ancient civilization now seemed pretty damned goofy. I looked at my new bride. Even bathed in moonlight, she looked pale.

"Maybe we should go back, Ranger," she whispered, as if she might wake up someone or *something.*

"Tyuonyi is just a bit further," I reassured her.

Truth be told, the noise my heart made clanging in my chest rivaled that of the Tin Man's in Oz. I was scared, but I didn't want her to know that. We walked on until we reached the gate to Tyuonyi, the largest Pueblo ruin in the canyon. Circular in shape, and standing one story high, the Pueblo once was three stories tall with over 400 rooms. In the center of the ruin were three small kivas. Shadows made them look like ominous black pits. Then things got weird...

"What was that?"

I don't know if it was me or Mary B who said it. The wind stilled. I began to hear faint murmurings. Shadowy images flitted about at the edges of my sight, but when I turned my head, they disappeared seamlessly into the landscape. Hushed chanting—

syllables of a dialect not of this world—emanated from the Pueblo walls.

My ESP gauge registered RUN LIKE HELL. The longer I stood in Tyuonyi, the tighter my sphincter got. Mary B grabbed my hand.

"Ranger, we have to go NOW!"

Her words, however hushed, were clarion calls to the spirits—the ones that'd risen from below, squeezing themselves through the sipapu. We turned to leave. What began as an orderly retreat, quickly turned into a wild-eyed, horses-from-a-burning-barn, run for your lives, bolt. I galloped ahead of Mary B. *Chivalry be damned.* We raced all the way back to our lodge, locked the front door, undressed, and climbed under the covers. In our small bedroom, we listened, hoping the spirits hadn't followed us home. That night, the hall lamp stayed lit.

Anasazi 1, Newlyweds 0.

…And that was the end of the romantic ruins sojourn.

#

Shortly after our moonlit ruins folly, autumn finally arrived. One frosty night in late October, Mary B and I were awakened by something on our roof.

"What was that?" Mary B asked, reclaiming the covers that mostly covered me.

"I don't know," I whispered.

Firelight shadows from the bedroom kiva pitter-patted across the viga beam ceiling, like Japanese shadow puppets. The thing on our roof started to eat, and for the next two hours, we listened to its guttural growls. *A mountain lion?* Every so often, it left the roof, only to return. Then I recalled how our neighbor in the adjoining lodge—a thick-mustachioed Ranger who listened to Jimmy Buffet at top volume—had a fondness for elk meat, and would toss dinner scraps out his kitchen window. Over time, the pile of bones and sinew grew, creating a tempting smorgasbord for any mountain lion on the dole.

The next morning, I rose early to a frigid room. I jump-started the fire, made coffee and hurried into my NPS uniform. I stepped outside, cupping a steaming mug of coffee. My breath condensed. Several inches of snow had fallen in the night. The canyon was cold and still. I walked around to the back of our cabin and crouched in the freshly fallen snow, looking for clues that might reveal the identity of our nocturnal visitor. And then I saw tracks. Imprinted in the snow were the unmistakable indentations of a large puma—four toes and a trapezoid-shaped palm—heading upslope away from our lodge. In their wake were splintered femurs, ribs and scapulas; testimony to the osseous inclinations of a hungry mountain lion.

#

Autumn in the canyon exited as quickly as it entered. Everyone's log pile shrank a notch or two. Thanksgiving gave way to Christmas in Frijoles Canyon—a tantalizing ensemble of sights, sounds and smells. A patina of frost greeted me each morning on my short jaunt to work. At night, Piñon fires burned in lodge kivas, swirling up sweet smelling smoke, which hung languidly between the walls of the canyon. Glowing holiday farolitos—paper bags weighted down with sand and lighted candles—lined walkways and parapet walls. Big-bulb Christmas lights dangled from portal porches and vigas, sending out beacons of colored light.

I acquired a Christmas tree permit from the US Forest Service, and on a bright but frigid December day, Mary B and I ventured deep into the Jemez Mountains in search of the perfect Christmas tree. It was our first Christmas as newlyweds. We cut down a small Douglas fir sapling poking out of a snow bank, and lashed it onto the roof of our Dodge Dart. When we got it home, it couldn't fit through the front door. The tree had what hairdressers might call "volume," and not the Donald Trump variety. Even with a trim, the Christmas bush obliterated a door and a window in our bedroom, and rendered the top two drawers of our dresser useless. Spatially arranging Christmas trees in an appropriate interior setting, is a skill that eludes me to this day.

For Bandelier's Christmas party, the Chief "volunteered" me to be St. Nick. As I stepped into a wide Santa suit, I wondered if the experience would be useful on my résumé. Strapping on a fake beard and practicing hardy HO HO HO's in the mirror, I grabbed a large sack of toys and lumbered through the snow to the administration building, where the festivities were underway. I sat on a wide, wooden chair in the middle of the room. The children of moms and dads I worked with sat at my feet, their eyes wide in wonderment. As I passed out toys, Santa also passed out sage advice.

"Tell your dad to never draw to an inside straight," I said to one boy, whose father was in our Friday night poker group.

"Tell your mom to bring more of those delicious oatmeal cookies to work," I whispered into a little girl's ear.

I followed these up with bellicose HO-HO-HO's. Being Santa, I figured, meant never having to say you're sorry.

#

January 1, 1983, Bandelier National Monument: I rose early and put on a pair of swim trunks. I prepared a pot of strong coffee, and as it percolated, laced up my Nike shoes. I wrapped up in a cotton, J.C. Penney bathrobe, filled a travel mug with syrupy black java, grabbed my plastic LA Dodger batting helmet, and stepped into a sub-freezing morning. Tiny, crystalline ice clouds swirled with each exhale. My nose hairs hurt. I took a route that crossed over an arched, stone bridge, very near the alcohol-fueled, Turkey vulture battle site. I turned down canyon, then veered off through the trees to a US Geological Gauging station—the site of Bandelier's inaugural Polar Bear gathering.

Over the Christmas holidays, Ranger Rick—the Ranger with the affinity for elk meat—asked me if I wanted to be in Bandelier's Polar Bear Club. I figured the number of people in the Canyon crazy enough to do something this stupid could be counted on one hand, and I was the thumb. So, I said yes. I didn't want Rick to be standing alone on the banks of Frijoles Creek, like a jilted Polar Bear at the altar of ice.

When I got to the Polar Bear site, I was surprised to see dozens of people huddled around, all in bathing suits and holding cushy bath towels. *Why didn't I bring a towel?* Reporters from Los Alamos mingled with would-be Polar Bears, snapping photos. Rick wore a heavy parka; his light-haired chicken legs stuck out from underneath it. His feet were ensconced in leather cowboy boots, and he wore a camouflaged hunter's cap. Next to him, a Pulaski and a tin pail were at the ready. I stood next to the Master of Ceremonies, shivering in my flimsy bathrobe and Dodger batting helmet, sipping hot coffee. Rick read the order of *Thalarctos maritimus* (Polar bear), smashed a hole in the ice with the Pulaski, gave a "No Guts, No Glory" Viking yell, and the floe party was on!

People entered the waist-high, icy pool two at a time, squatting in brain-numbing water for an interminable sixty seconds. After a minute, Polar Bear trainees were offered a choice; fully submerse, or get doused with a bucket of creek water. Most chose submersion. Finally, it was my turn. I'd put it off long enough. I walked barefoot over the snow to the hole, and peered in. Thick chunks of blue ice bobbed in the water.

"Your turn, Dutton," Rick said, smiling.

I hesitated. About the time my frozen toes left the bank, I wished they hadn't. The cold water seized my groin like glacial vice grips. My gonads shrank to the size of lima beans. My body was being pierced by zillions of tiny icy knives. *Why did I agree to this?*

After a protracted minute, I submerged. My face was paralyzed. I surfaced with an agonal respiration. Rick gave me the full measure of the bucket for good measure. *Thanks, Ranger Rick.* I pulled myself out of the frozen hole, and slid across the snow like a baby harp seal eluding a club-wielding Russian. I tried to lace up my shoes, but my fingers didn't work. I slogged back to our lodge and stood in the kitchen, shivering. Icy creek water puddled onto the flagstone floor. I needed a hot shower, but as luck would have it, the water main which provided water to the canyon had frozen the night before. Hot water wasn't to be had.

"Why don't you get out of your wet clothes, Ranger," Mary B suggested.

She shook her head incredulously as she fetched some towels. Everything except my Dodger helmet fell in a wet heap. I climbed into bed, and set the electric blanket on HIGH. By halftime of the Rose Bowl, I could feel my toes. By halftime of the Orange Bowl, I felt human.

Polar Bears 1, Dutton 0.

The first day of 1983 proved eventful. The next 364 days would likewise follow suit.

#

Picture this: A fecund January storm double-parks over northern New Mexico. Pregnant with Gulf moisture, it spawns several feet of snow. A heavyset man trudges through it. He enters the VC, and stamps his feet, shaking off snow. Except for the somnolent sounds of a crackling fire, the building is silent.

The man walks to the information desk, but no one greets him. The roaring fire beckons. He walks to it, hoping to borrow its warmth. Another man occupies a couch in front of the fire; his boots are propped on a wooden table in front of the hearth. His head is tilted down. He is asleep with arms folded across his chest, snoring.

The heavyset man looks down at the sleeping man. He pauses, then places a strong hand on the man's shoulder.

I open my eyes, and stare up at my boss, the Chief of Interpretation for Bandelier National Monument.

"Shouldn't be sleeping on the job, Dutton," the Chief says, in a deep drawl.

"Yes, sir."

"I came over to relieve you for lunch."

"Thank you."

I wipe drool from the corner of my mouth, grab my parka and Stetson, and head out into swirling, shin-high snow. *Poorly played Dutton, poorly played.*

Okay, now picture this: A man enters the VC, stomps snow from his boots and tries to shake off the cold. He walks to the information desk. No one is there to greet him. A roaring fire beckons. A heavyset man lays sprawled, his shiny shoes propped on a wooden table in front of the fire. His arms are folded across his chest. His lips flap noisily as air escapes.

The man peers down at the heavier man asleep on the couch. He pauses, then places a strong hand on the man's shoulder.

The Chief opens his eyes, and looks up.

"Shouldn't be sleeping on the job," I say.

"You're right."

"Thanks for the lunch break, Chief."

The Chief rises, gathers his parka and Stetson, and heads for the door. He turns. "Nice fire, Dutton," he says, then opens the door and ventures into an arctic white mass.

Nice fire Indeed. It put us both to sleep!

#

In early January 1983, word came down from on-high that I would be let go, ostensibly because of budget cuts. My winter seasonal job was supposed to run through April. I told myself it wasn't because of my job performance, even though I was caught snoozing on the job.

On a dreary, cold January morning, about a week before the Super Bowl, Mary B and I loaded the last of our modest belongings into a 4 x 6 U-Haul trailer, filling up 140 cubit feet of space. As newlyweds, we were still trying to figure out the allocation of work, particularly when it came to moving. Having worked as a mover one summer, I felt qualified to oversee all the packing. Mary B, of course, did not see it that way. We eventually worked out a system whereby she packed and I loaded. It seemed to work. When the last box was stuffed into the U-Haul, Mary B emerged wearing bright yellow moon boots I got her for Christmas. They stayed on her feet all the way to the far side of the Mojave Desert.

I fired up the Dodge, and we ascended out of an icy Frijoles Canyon. We waved goodbye to Nakai as we passed the stables. His head was down as he tore at a hay bale. We rounded the big turn at the top of the mesa, and glimpsed the Rio Grande far below, shimmering in the winter sun. We passed the fire tower, where I feasted on beans and sunsets, except, of course, when Mary B was standing next to me. We turned right onto NM 4, and dropped down out of the Jemez Mountains. An hour and a half later, we negotiated the "The Big I" interchange in Albuquerque, and once again headed into Basin and Range country, setting a course for Gallup, 140 miles to the west.

Driving along, I reflected back on my time spent between the towering, tuff walls of Frijoles Canyon. Bandelier was where I was weaned as an NPS pup. It was my teat. I would miss it. We had enough gas money to get us to Monterey (her parents were taking us in), and maybe some extra nickels for a green chile cheeseburger or two, but not much more. I looked over at Mary B asleep with her moon boots on. I smiled. I'd found the girl willing to share a fire tower with. And my career? Well, that was the shiftless nature of being an NPS seasonal Park Ranger—you just never knew where you'd end up next.

Sand, Surf and Fog

June 1, 1888 – Very Foggy
~ Point Reyes Lighthouse, Keeper's Log

In late January 1983, we moved in with Mary B's parents in Monterey, California, and set up shop on a couple of kissing couches in their living room. An El Niño weather pattern (Spanish, meaning "run for high ground"), dropped three and a half feet of rain along California's central and northern coasts, making it one of the sloshiest winters on record.

Mary's older brother, Jeff, a rabid 49ers' fan, and a pressman at the Monterey Herald, finagled me a job in the circulation department delivering newspapers. My route covered Fort Ord, a sandy Army outpost a few miles north of Monterey, where, as a pimply-faced basic training private 10 years earlier, I'd learned to shoot an M-16, and march in a straight line. When I wasn't learning to shoot, I also pulled guard duty at the nearby Presidio (Spanish, meaning fort), which overlooked Monterey Bay. As I ambled about in well-nourished fog with an empty rifle, I was serenaded by barking, bachelor bull sea lions that hung out on the Coast Guard pier jutting into Monterey Bay. Mostly though, I ran off horny high school kids necking in the backseats of their parent's Volvos. *National defense man!*

After I finished my deliveries, I often parked the Herald truck on a hill overlooking the rifle ranges. I'd stare out at the dark ocean and recall the drill sergeants' debauched marching cadences:

...I wish all the ladies
Were holes in a road
And I was a dump truck
I'd fill 'em with my load.
Your left, your left, your left, right, left...

#

Shortly after we arrived in Monterey, Mary B found work at a swanky art shop in downtown Carmel. Of course, everything in Carmel was swanky. With her degree from Cal Poly in Applied Art and Design, she knew her way around a framed print. Some mornings, after an all-nighter at the Herald, I'd meet her for coffee and donuts across from the store, when she was on break. Sitting on an ornate park bench, we'd conjure stories about the well-heeled men and women coming and going in their Jaguars and Mercedes along Ocean Avenue. As the donuts disappeared, we talked about our future, which at the time seemed very uncertain.

Following an abbreviated winter stint at Bandelier, I rushed out applications for summer Park Ranger jobs to Joshua Tree National Monument and Point Reyes National Seashore. As the Ides of March rolled in, and with bupkis on the NPS radar, I was getting worried.

#

At this point friends and neighbors, you might want to grab a cold Oly from the fridge, as I need to detour into the titillating world of federal employment—subject matter of dirt-like dryness.

Anyone who ever applied for a federal government job during the 1970's and 1980's, knows all too well the joys of filling out Standard Form 171, Application for Federal Employment. The 171 is an omnibus form. It *needs* to know everything about your life—foreign language aptitude, special interests, hobbies, typing ability, work history (starting with kindergarten), training, honors, awards, education level, military service (if any), and where you've had sex (especially germane if public land was used for such pursuits).

Filling out a 171 required Zen-like introspection, especially when it came to assessing your skill level. For example, I know I can row a dinghy, but does that make me qualified to pilot a patrol boat. Why, hell yes it does! Did I occasionally leg out a double for experience that really only amounted to a base hit? Bet your ass I did. After all, I was competing for scarce, Federal Park Ranger jobs with the single biggest demographic in American history—baby boomers.

As if the 171 wasn't onerous enough, federal agencies usually requested supplemental information, called KSA's— knowledge, skills and abilities. Rank and file called them **K**now **S**omeone in **A**uthority, or **K**iss **S**omeone's **A**ss. Examples of KSA's might be, Ability to Communicate Effectively both Orally and in Writing or Knowledge of Park Operations. I didn't know anyone in the Park Service with enough cache to get me an entry level job, and butt-puckering, well that never agreed with me either. So I became a federal angler, casting out 171's. In the words of one-time US Forest Service employee Norman Maclean, I hoped a fish would rise up.

#

Early one morning in late spring, the phone at my in-laws house rang. I picked it up on the third ring.

"Yes, this is David Dutton," I answered, sleepily. I was coming off a twelve hour shift at the Herald and had just lain down on the couch. Suddenly, I was wide awake.

"Yes, I'm still interested."

"Beginning when?"

"Is housing available?"

I hung up the phone. Mary B stood in the hallway in her red fuzzy bathrobe.

"Have you ever been to Point Reyes National Seashore?" I asked.

A huge smile arced across her face.

#

In early May, we packed up both bugs, waved goodbye to Monterey, and caravanned north up a ridiculously crowded US 101. We crossed the Golden Gate Bridge (which is not golden by the way), and turned onto bandy-legged Hwy 1, following the craggy coastline of the Marin headlands for twenty-five miles, until we saw the entrance sign for Point Reyes National Seashore. We pulled in, and for the next seven months, called the place home.

Our NPS singlewide trailer rested on stacked cinder blocks thirty feet from the infamous San Andreas Fault. In 1906, when the fault had a little itch, it leveled San Francisco. The San Andreas Fault (SAF in geologic parlance), is the dividing line between two massive tectonic plates—the North American and the Pacific. Point Reyes sits on the Pacific plate. Studies have shown that slippage, or horizontal movement along the SAF's northern zone, has been about a centimeter a year for the past twenty centuries. Two thousand years ago, Jesus Christ and I could have faced each other across the fault line. Today, there'd be 167 feet of distance between us.

My duty station was the Bear Valley Visitor Center—a converted ranch house and barn—harking back to the heyday when Point Reyes was an international cattle and dairy ranching community. The interpretive staff at the Seashore was a cadre of Rangers who knew their jobs, yet never took themselves too seriously. Our supervisor, Greg, was easygoing, with a thick, curly beard and an earring in one lobe. He was a fungus guy. On his days off, he roamed the seashore like a Hobbit, bagging mushrooms, especially the meaty and flavorful chanterelles. After a soggy winter, fungi were plentiful in the mixed evergreen forests of Point Reyes. When in season, Chanterelles adorned the dinner plates of San Francisco's finest restaurants.

On my first day at Point Reyes National Seashore, I reported to work, spit-shined and creased.

"Damn Dutton," Greg said, looking me over, "you look like a real Ranger." He handed me the keys to the government truck. "Go see the Seashore. Get to know the place. Just be back before quitting time."

I hopped into a government truck (a Chevy relic with the stick shift on the steering column), and drove by our trailer to pick up Mary B. Fifteen minutes later, we looked out on Tomales Bay, where Great White sharks go to do the horizontal bop. On this morning, the tide was out, exposing shiny mud flats, pockmarked with small pools of seawater. Egrets with appliance-white plumage and stilty legs probed the puddles with long beaks, looking for fishes that missed the last tide bus out of town.

The road skirted the western edge of Tomales Bay, and soon we reached Inverness—a bohemian enclave of weathered clapboard storefronts, funky boutiques, and a restaurant called the Gray Whale. Some of the Ranger's wives worked at the restaurant, serving up pizzas. Mary B would end up working there as well. That was the thing about Park Ranger's spouses— they would try and get jobs at the places where their husbands worked to help make needs meet. We ordered some sandwiches to go, and pushed on, taking the road to Tomales Point, the spear tip of Point Reyes National Seashore.

As I double-clutched up a small rise, Mary B asked, "What's that over there, Ranger?" She pointed to a ridgeline. I pulled the truck over. Four-legged creatures with crowns on their heads stared back us.

"They look like deer," I said, except they had palmate antlers, like those on a moose, and spots along their flanks, like fawns. Turns out they were Fallow deer, a non-native species from the Mediterranean, that were introduced onto the peninsula by ranchers for sport hunting, before it became a National Seashore in 1962. We admired them for awhile, then continued to the Tomales Point trailhead. We got out and hiked north along a pig trail. The sun had ladled a hole in the soupy fog, and the Pacific Ocean loomed large below us. Incessant winds boxed the ocean, scarring it with wavy white lines. Low, hardy shrubs and ankle-high grasses eked out a living along this windswept, rocky outcropping. We trudged on for another mile or so, our faces getting wind-slapped. As we turned to head back, a splash of color caught my eye.

"Mary, look at your shoes!"

She looked down. Stretched across her shoelaces was a garter snake, thick as the long end of a pool cue, with beautiful red, white and gray stripes running the length of its foot-long body. Mary B reached down and gently picked up the snake. It looked more like a colorful, pregnant shoelace, than a snake. We admired it for awhile, then Mary B let it go. The serpent glided effortlessly across the low grasses, and disappeared under a rock. After dinner that night, we looked the snake up in a guide book. Apparently Mary B had in her hands an endangered species—a San Francisco garter snake—and the only place in the world that it calls home is the Point Reyes peninsula.

We hiked back to the parking lot, ate our deli sandwiches, then drove toward the Point Reyes headlands. As we headed west, we began smelling what the Service called the Pastoral Zone—verdant pastureland stretching 10 miles to the Pacific Ocean. From afar, the undulating landscape looked like green, pool table felt. Black and white dairy cows with bulging udders kept their wet noses to it, as if looking for lost contact lenses. Point Reyes once boasted the largest dairy industry in California. Watching the cows munch on succulent grass stalks, brought back haunting memories of the skeletal stilts I'd seen rooting in the dust along the Rio Grande.

A half-hour later, we reached the farthest edge of the Point Reyes headlands. I got out and looked down at the crashing Pacific Ocean hundreds of feet below. Baying California Sea lions looked like fuzzy brown jellybeans with flippers, as they jockeyed for the best rocks to rest their massive bulk on. We walked a short distance to the Point Reyes Lighthouse Visitor Center. Scores of binocular-clad visitors crowded the observation deck, scanning the wide, blue Pacific like Captain Ahab's, searching for California gray whale spouts.

During their 12,000 mile roundtrip journey between the Bering Sea and the warm lagoons of Mexico, California gray whales come close to Point Reyes, making it the Mecca for whale watching along the entire west coast of North America.

The lighthouse itself rests on a dynamited rock shelf three hundred feet above the surf. Thirty stories of concrete steps connect it to the VC. Point Reyes is the second foggiest place in North America. First place honors goes to Newfoundland. The lighthouse first became operational in 1870, and used oil lamps and a nifty French crystal lens to warn mariners to stay the hell away. A steam powered fog horn was also employed.

In 1975, the U.S. Coast guard retired the historic lighthouse, and replaced it with something fully automated. Looking out at the ocean swirling around Point Reyes, it's easy to see why the peninsula is such a navigational hazard for mariners. Over the centuries, scores of ships have French kissed it, virtually all with disastrous consequences.

During their shifts at the lighthouse, Rangers negotiate concrete steps going to and from the VC, often in windy and wet conditions. Wind speeds of 133 mph have been recorded at Point Reyes, and sixty mph winds are not uncommon. In the coming months, my calves, thighs and lungs would feel the burn of those climbs. By the end of my stint at Point Reyes though, I bounded up the steps like Rocky Balboa running up the stairs of the Philadelphia Museum of Art.

A late afternoon sun glinted off the ocean as we climbed into the truck for the 45-minute drive back to Bear Valley. Even though we'd spent the day exploring, I knew we'd only scratched the surface. With eighty miles of coastline, and 32,000 acres of congressionally designated wilderness, Point Reyes was a big sandbox to play in. There would be other adventures. I was sure of that.

#

With each passing day, Mary B and I discovered that we were not the only tenants occupying the NPS single-wide trailer we called home. Earwigs, mice, and raccoons were also frequent guests. A spirited Western flycatcher also had the same address as we did. Flycatchers usually nest in tree cavities, but this mom preferred the narrow sill of our bedroom window. She'd constructed her nest of soft lichens and conifer needles. At night, we turned off the bedroom light, and peeked at our feathered neighbor through a tattered, rusty screen. She stared back with unblinking eyes.

One summer morning, the shell-ensconced embryos she was incubating broke free, and rose up, wet and hungry. After that, she made countless trips to the nest, stuffing squishy insects down her chick's yawning beaks. At night, when it was time to rest, there she was, ever vigilant, watching over her tiny brood. *If I were her, I'd be on my second gin and tonic, and sucking on a menthol!*

#

If I were a bird, I'd want to be at Point Reyes. Nearly half of North America's bird species have made an appearance at Point Reyes at one time or another. Ornithologists think that because Point Reyes juts into the Pacific for ten miles, it makes an inviting layover for birds using the Pacific Flyway—an avian interstate, only without diamond lanes and traffic cops.

Of the nearly 500 bird species observed at Point Reyes, I grew to like the Acorn Woodpecker the best. Not to be confused with a Peckerwood—a Southernism reserved for dipshits that never use turn signals—Acorn Woodpeckers are hoarders of the highest order. As their name implies, they collect bushels of acorns and pincushion them into tree trunks for later use. These "granaries" are fiercely defended by other thug Acorn Woodpeckers with ominous beaks and brass knuckles. Watching these gregarious birds stuffing acorns into holes reminded me of women telephone operators in those grainy 1940s documentaries, plugging wire leads into holes in the switchboards in front of them.

#

Other than the abundant bird life at Point Reyes, it is probably best known for its omnipresent fog. It consumes everything—light, sound, even thought.

Picture this: It's nighttime. Except for owls and drunks at last call, the world is asleep. Fog creeps across the land, shrouding it like wildfire smoke. A tall California bay laurel tree with arching branches stands like a sentinel over a tin-roofed trailer. The advancing fog suffocates the tree with water vapor. Fat, watery droplets soon distill out of the fog and plummet to the trailer below, ringing it up with splashy gunshots. Sleep is impossible. The unsynchronized drip, drip, drip continues unabated, like a leaky faucet, all night long. Poe had ravens. Point Reyes has fog.

And so, following another fog induced, drippy hoedown-on-the roof, I pulled myself out of bed and shuffled to the kitchen. I fired up a pot of coffee, and stuffed two strawberry pop tarts into the toaster. After breakfast, I put on a clean uniform, laced up my boots, and set out for the Bear Valley VC, a quarter mile away. The morning sun riddled holes in the fog, creating smoky spirals that radiated off everything wet. As I walked through the wet grass, I was preoccupied with the thought of our last It's-It sitting in the freezer. Given the choice between a cold Oly and a vanilla ice cream confection, sandwiched between oatmeal cookies smothered in milk chocolate, I'd take the It's-It.

When I arrived at the VC, Boy Scouts were playing grabass in the parking lot. Their leaders—grown men in kerchiefs and knee-high socks—waited nervously outside the VC like expectant fathers, hoping to score a coveted backcountry campsite. The NPS doled them out on a first-come, first-serve basis.

Allan, one of my cohorts, pulled into the VC parking lot, narrowly missing a scout's backpack. Allan was a permanent Park Ranger, and a seasoned interpreter. He stepped out of his car, balancing pastries in one hand and his lunch in the other. Allan bivouacked in the old Coast Guard barracks, out at the lighthouse.

"Good morning," I called out.

"It's foggier than hell out at the lighthouse," Allan shouted back. "I almost hit a cow."

"Try explaining that to the Chief," I said. I always thought it amazing, given Allan's race car proclivities, that he didn't have a cow part as a hood ornament.

I unlocked the VC, and the scouts rushed in like the tide. Allan set down the goodies, and immediately snatched up the backcountry ledger. The scout elders followed him like he was the backcountry pied piper. As Allan worked the backcountry reservations book, I busied myself with the minutiae of opening the VC—stocking books, guides, pamphlets, readying the cash register and making coffee. The scouts milled about the VC, looking at the stuffed animal mounts on the wall. They began asking questions, most of which fell into either of two categories—dangerous or gross.

"Ranger, have you ever seen a Great White shark?"

"Ranger, can you eat those slimy yellow worms you see crawling all over the place?"

"Ranger, what are those funny black birds you see flying around sticking things into trees?" *Ah. Smart lad. A naturalist in the making.*

Allan hunched over the backcountry journal, scribbling and erasing furiously with a stubby pencil. The scout leaders crowded around, shouting their preferred campsites. As their availability steadily dwindled, tensions mounted. It was painfully obvious there were more scouts than campsites to accommodate them all. Some poor troop would go home empty handed. Allan became visibly flummoxed. He scrawled, erased and pecked at the backcountry ledger like a barnyard hen. Finally, he slammed the pencil down, looked up, and in a stentorian voice, proclaimed: "THE CAMPGROUNDS ARE FUCKED!"

The VC went morgue. Everyone stared at Ranger Allan. His round cheeks looked like half-filled balloons. He covered his mouth with his hand, the equivalent of the Dutch boy with his finger in the comic dike. But the dike burst. Laughter spilled out of Allan in belly-shaking waves. The scout leaders stepped away from the information desk, dumbfounded. Their young protégés however, found Allan's comment hilarious, and laughed right along with him. I did, too. Allan tried valiantly to rally. He paused, surfaced for air, and managed a professional correction.

"I'm sorry," he apologized, "the campgrounds are full!"

Despite Allan's correction, everyone reeled from the F-bomb shockwave. After things died down a bit, I approached Allan.

"What the hell was that all about?" I asked, handing him a cup of coffee.

"Well," Allan began, "first I meant to say the campgrounds were full. Then I changed my mind and meant to say the campgrounds were booked. Then I panicked, and put the two words together."

"Try not to get those words mixed up again," I said, laughing.

#

Late in the afternoon of an already hectic Saturday, Allan walked over to the VC phone and began dialing.

"Who are you calling?" I asked.

"Shhh!" he said, placing a forefinger in front of a mischievously wide grin.

"Hello, is this the Pt. Rayless Lighthouse?" Allan slurred. "Can you ell me when the whalesses nest on the rocks?" Allan hiccupped into the receiver. "We have a pool go-go-go, goin'," he stuttered, "and my boss keeps insissiting that the whalesses are mating now." His impersonation of a soused businessman on a wine tasting tour of Napa Valley was spot on. There was a pronounced pause. Allan listened. His body shook as he struggled to hold back a laugh.

"What? What do you mean whalesses don't nest? Of course they fucking do!"

"What?"

"What's a mamammmal?"

I almost pissed.

At straight up five, we locked the VC doors and closed shop. Allan got into his car, and headed for the lighthouse and wayward dairy cows. I walked back to the trailer for a well deserved It's-It. I bounded up the front porch steps of our trailer and flung open the front door.

"I'm home," I announced, like Ricky Ricardo.

I opened the freezer and peered in.

"Mary B, have you seen the It's-It?" I asked, pushing aside a bag of frozen peas.

There was a muffled response from the rear of the trailer. Walking down the narrow hallway, I glanced into the bathroom. On the counter was a torn It's-It wrapper. *She's eaten it!*

Mary B was busy putting clothes away when I entered the bedroom. On the nightstand next to the bed, was a half eaten It's-It. She looked at me, bulgy-eyed. Her mouth was full. *No doubt with the other half of my It's-It.* Quick as a gunslinger, she grabbed the It's-It from the nightstand, and rushed past me down the hall. She raced down the porch steps and into the yard. I was in hot pursuit.

"No, no, stop!" I pleaded.

We raced around the trailer. On the second lap, I finally caught up to her, just as she swallowed what was left of the It's-it. Mary B laughed so hard she choked. Chocolate smeared her lips and chin.

"I can't believe you did that," I said, out of breath.

At that same moment, Ms. Flycatcher flew overhead with a juicy beetle clasped in her tiny bill. She divvied up the beetle and patiently fed some to each of her yawning chicks, then flew off in search of another meal.

At least in the flycatcher family, they share.

#

Throughout the summer of 1983, oodles of plump blackberries hung like purple orbs from hedgerows all over the Point Reyes peninsula. On my days off, Mary B and I plucked them from spiky vines until our hands were stained amethyst. We hauled them back to our trailer in plastic buckets and dumped them into cooking pots. For weeks after, sugary aromas wafted from our trailer, and mingled with the incessant fog. Pint jars of homemade blackberry jam soon lined the shelves of our meager larder. For breakfast, we enjoyed plump blackberries with our cornflakes, and at night, blackberry pie or cobbler for dessert.

In early fall, during my walks to the VC, I began noticing bulbous, shiny green apples, dangling from a two-story apple tree growing outside the Superintendent's office. After dinner one night, I mentioned it to Mary B.

"Mary B," I said, leaning back in my dining chair, "I sure could go for an apple pie."

There was a pause, then Mary B said, "That tree outside the Superintendent's office is loaded with apples."

"Yeah, but we don't have a ladder."

"I think the maintenance guy next door has one. Why not borrow his?" Clearly, Mary B had a plan.

"You mean Hoot?"

"Yeah, whatever his name is."

"Good idea. I'll ask him."

The next morning I saw our neighbor taking out his garbage. Hoot had scrawny, leathery arms that looked like they belonged on a Galapagos tortoise.

"Morning," I hollered.

"Mornin'," Hoot answered back. A cigarette, ninety-eight percent spent, clung stubbornly to his lower lip.

"Hey Hoot, do you think maybe I can borrow your ladder?"

Hoot slammed the lid down on his trashcan. "Sure. What you needin' it for? Gonna do some apple thievin'? The Sup's tree is loaded with 'em," he grinned, showing teeth the color of dried mustard.

"Ladder's on the side of the trailer. Grab it when you need it. Bring me back a few apples."

"Will do," I said.

There was no moon the night Mary B and I slipped out the front door of our trailer. Armed with Hoot's rickety wooden ladder and some five gallon buckets, we looked more like window washers than apple thieves. I carried the ladder, and Mary B carried the buckets. Minutes later, we squatted under the apple tree outside the Superintendent's office. Headlights from passing cars out on Hwy 1 splashed on the tall windows of the headquarters building. I placed the ladder against a stout limb and climbed a few rungs. Several apples fell off and thudded on the soft grass below. Some however, hit Mary B on the head.

"Damnit Ranger, watch out!" she whispered, hoarsely.

Mary B skittered and dodged, collecting apples in the five gallon buckets while I continued the shakedown. Soon, our buckets were full. When a pair of high beams lit up the parking lot in front of the headquarters building, we dropped the buckets and scurried for cover, like cockroaches in the glare of a porch light. One of the seashore's law enforcement Rangers lived just down the road from our trailer. *Did he see us carrying the ladder and buckets, dressed as apple Ninjas?* He was a zealous sort though, with a fierce Barney Fife streak. If he saw us thieving taxpayer apples, he'd rat on us for sure. I'd have a lot of explaining to do to the Sup. Could even get fired.

After several tense minutes, the vehicle backed out and drove off. We quickly retrieved the ladder and buckets, and shuffled back home with our booty. Sitting at the kitchen table, I admired the night's haul. I picked a big apple from the bucket, and bit deeply into its flesh. The apple snapped hard, sending juicy rivulets across the kitchen table. I wiped my chin.

"They're delicious!"

And so, for weeks after the heist, tantalizing pastry aromas drifted from the Dutton trailer, teasing neighborhood dogs, wildlife, or just about anything with a sniffer. Not long after the heist, I presented Hoot with an 'Apple thievin' pie for the use of his ladder. He snatched it from my hands, and disappeared into his trailer like a squirrel with a nut.

#

One afternoon, shortly after the apple heist, the rotary phone at the Bear Valley VC rang.

"Point Reyes National Seashore, Bear Valley Visitor Center, can I help you?" I answered.

"Ranger, Red Ruby got burned up!" It was Mary B, and she was distraught.

"What?" I heard wailing sirens in the background.

"I did the grocery shopping…and was driving home, and… Red Ruby caught fire. The tow truck guy said…something about a leaky fuel line…"

Are you okay?"

"Yes…" I heard sobs.

"I'm on Sir Francis Boulevard. Please hurry."

"I'm on my way."

I hung up the phone, and told Greg I had an emergency. I ran home to our trailer, hopped into my bug and headed east on Sir Francis Drake Boulevard. I drove until I saw flashing red lights. Fire trucks were parked haphazardly in the street. Their thick yellow fire hoses crisscrossed the boulevard. Melting flares littered the street like discarded carmine cigars. Off to the side, Red Ruby smoldered.

I walked over to Mary B, who sat on the curb. Grocery bags with green, leafy things sticking out the top were on the sidewalk next to her. I put an arm around her trembling shoulders. We watched the tow truck doctor load the charred remains of Red Ruby onto a flatbed gurney and wheel her away. *There goes a lot of good memories.* I put the groceries in the back seat of my bug, and we drove back to our trailer in silence. The Dutton motorpool was now down to one VW.

One week later, I sat with my father-in-law in the sales manager's office of a Mazda dealership in Seaside, California. Dark paneled walls were adorned with framed "Salesmen of the Year" plaques.

"Where do you work, young man?" The car salesman asked.

"I'm a Park Ranger at Point Reyes National Seashore, sir," I answered.

"You know, I always wanted to be a Park Ranger," he said.

I smiled. *I don't think so, peckerwood.* Sitting across from me was a man with enough bling around his fatty neck to sink a ship. I wasn't convinced that earning $12,000 per annum—which is what I was knocking down at the time—fit into his lifestyle.

Wayne, my father-in-law, winced as he inked his name on the co-sign line—a 17% APR car loan. It would cost $150 a month. When you live in a government trailer and eat blackberries and apples for sustenance, that's a king's ransom.

#

One of the perks of living in a National Park (or a National Seashore), is that you get to see and experience things that visitors ordinarily do not. For us, it was the Point Reyes Morgan Horse Ranch—a facility where the NPS breeds Morgan horses for use in national parks. The NPS kept Morgan ponies in a large corral behind the VC. After dinner, Mary B and I would stroll over, and feed them handfuls of blackberries that stained their hairy noses purple. Whenever they saw us coming, they'd make a beeline for the fence.

During our brief fall-winter layover at Bandelier, Mary B and I enjoyed horseback rides into Bandelier's backcountry on one such Morgan horse that was born, raised and trained at Point Reyes National Seashore. His name was Cid, and he was chestnut-colored with a white blaze on his forehead. Cid was wide and sturdy, with a gait as smooth as a Cadillac DeVille. The horse I rode—boney kneed *Nakai*—was a Navajo wildling, with a gait that would chip your teeth. If Nakai were a car, he'd probably be a Kia.

One evening, I had this crazy notion that I'd ride one of them. I asked Mary B to coax one of the young fillies over to the fence. As the horse muzzled juicy blackberries in Mary B's outstretched palm, I quietly climbed the corral fence, and leapt. From out of the sky, one hundred and sixty pounds dropped onto the Morgan's stout spine. She turned her head sideways and reared back. When she did, I could see the whites of her bulgy, terror-filled eyes. She bolted like an Olympic sprinter out of the starting blocks...*this is not going to end well.*

"Ride 'em, cowboy," Mary B whooped, as I galloped past, holding the horse's mane the way a senior citizen grips a walker. The filly galloped faster and faster. My eyes watered. If she ran straight, I hoped, I might be able to apply the brakes. I dug in my heels and pulled hard on her mane, but there was no stopping her. It was clear that horse and rider were not as one. Finally, she zigged right, and I left. The ground came up fast. I bounced, and bounced again, and possibly a third time, finally rolling to a stop, face down in Point Reyes granitic dirt. Mary B ran over to me.

"Are you okay, Ranger?"

Her voice conveyed concern, yet was also laced with, "Why does he do shit like this?" I rolled over, rubbing my ribs.

"There she goes," Mary B said. Minus her tormentor, the filly galloped spiritedly, tail flagging in the wind.

A few weeks later I told the horse ranch manager about my episode with the young horse, although in my telling, I was much more like John Wayne.

"Are you talking about those horses in the corral behind the VC?" she asked.

"Yeah," I nodded.

She began to laugh. "They've never had a rider on their backs." She couldn't stop laughing. Tears welled in her eyes. She struggled to breathe.

"They're too young," she gasped. "Only thing they've ever had on their backs are flies."

I'll be dipped in shit!

#

One day, not long after we bought our new Mazda truck, the sun shined on our trailer. *A message from the Gods?* Mary B was in the kitchen cooking breakfast. I poured a cup of Folgers, and sat down at the kitchen table in my boxer shorts and long sleeve Cal Poly shirt. A piece of paper lay on the table—an NPS job vacancy bulletin. Someone had highlighted in lime green a GS-0025/04 Park Ranger vacancy at Mammoth Cave National Park, Kentucky. I looked over at Mary B.

"Did you highlight this?" I asked.

Mary B nodded, then flipped some bacon in the fry pan.

"You seriously want me to apply for a Park Ranger job in Kentucky?"

"Why not? It's a permanent position isn't it?"

I didn't like having a conversation with her back, although her shiny brunette hair looked nice. She was right though. It was a permanent position, one with benefits. It's what we both wanted. But Kentucky? Banjo music from *Deliverance* plinked in my head. I changed the subject.

"C'mon, Mary, the sun's out. Let's go for a drive."

"Where?"

"Limantour Beach."

"I thought Limantour Road got washed out during El Niño?"

"It did. Greg said there's a fire road that goes around the washout though. He said the road's a little curvy, but passable. There's a locked gate, but he let me borrow his key. We'll have the whole place to ourselves!"

Limantour Beach was a very popular destination with visitors to Point Reyes. With the main access road washed out though, the only way to access the beach was on foot—an eight mile, one way trek from the Bear Valley VC.

"Well then, let's go," Mary B said.

Calling the fire road "a little curvy," as Greg described it, was a little like calling a Sumo wrestler "a little pudgy." After hairpin twists and taffy-like turns, we butted up against a cattle gate. Using Greg's key I unlocked it, and we drove on a short distance, through forests of pungent Douglas fir and Bishop Pine, until there was a break in the canopy. It afforded us a view of the cobalt Pacific far below. There was no fog. *Unbelievable!*

I pulled over, and we got out. The ground underfoot was spongy and moist. I looked down and saw something yellow just as Mary B's heel came down on it. She didn't see it. Her foot slid across the leaf litter like socks across linoleum.

"What was that?" she asked, regaining her balance.

She'd accidentally trampled the seashore's iconic, terrestrial invertebrate—a Banana Slug—and felt horrible about it. Banana slugs, like clams, mussels and oysters, are mollusks, except they don't have a shell. In dry times, they coat their bodies with sticky mucus so they don't dry out. Banana slugs can grow up to ten inches, although most only reach the size of a Garcia Vega cigar— about six inches long. Banana slugs are decomposers, sucking up leaves and animal waste like Hoover vacuums, and recycling it back into soil. *Without decomposers like Banana slugs, friends and neighbors, we'd all be up to our collective asses in organicalness.*

We got back into the truck and drove on. We were on the windward side of Inverness ridge, and could smell the salty pungency of the Pacific Ocean. For some reason, it made me think about all those corporate chemists toiling away in their labs, trying to reproduce the smell of a beach in full bloom, just so folks could spritz their living rooms after Pico the Chihuahua did the poop scoot across the shag carpet. Good luck.

"Look at that!" Mary B suddenly shouted.

A lanky bobcat with a long-eared hare dangling from its jaws ran along the road next to the Mazda. The tailless kitty easily clocked twenty-five mph. It jaunted along for another quarter mile, before veering into a patch of thick chaparral.

Where the ocean put up its palm, we parked and got out. I immediately heard the familiar sounds of beach warfare—curling breakers pummeling a stubborn beach, followed by loud hissing as they retreated out to sea. We crested a small dune marginally held together with spiky beach grass, and took in the wide Pacific Ocean, set out for before us like a blue, vinyl tablecloth. A brilliant sun transformed its surface into glimmering jewels. The jagged Farallon Islands, twenty miles out to sea, pierced the waters like shark fins.

Virgin sand, untouched by human soles, stretched for miles in either direction. Piles of driftwood polished smooth by gritty winds lay in clustered heaps, as did tangles of desiccated Bull kelp. Clouds of tiny, black flies buzzed over them. In the surf, itty-bitty Plovers with pointy beaks motored on scaly toes just ahead of roiling foam. As the breakers reversed course, the Plovers gave chase, probing for hidden crustaceans like feathered drill rigs. Pelicans, the B-52's of the avian world, soared on airstreams in front of cresting waves, as ubiquitous gulls argued in the skies overhead. Salty ocean spray vaporized with each crashing wave, leaving briny residues on our skin.

The spirit of Robinson Crusoe overcame me, and I abandoned my clothes at the base of a dune. *Who hasn't taken off all their clothes when they've been alone in nature? Anyone?* Mrs. Crusoe, ever practical, kept her clothes on, and applied sunscreen. A snug ball cap kept her long, brown hair from whipping her face. We walked hand in hand along the spit. Uppity waves erased our footprints as we walked.

"Ranger, come look at this," Mary B shouted into the howling wind. She was stooped over, holding something in her hand. It resembled a broken piece of cereal bowl.

"What is it?" I asked.

She turned the object over. Its white edges were worn smooth. Intricate blue markings—similar to those found on saucers and tea cups in expensive Chinese restaurants—adorned both sides.

Remember all those ships that had run-ins with the rocky headlands of Point Reyes? Many were Spanish galleons, loaded to the gills with niceties from China, like silks and porcelain, possibly from the Ming Dynasty dating back to the 1300's. Their disgorged cargoes were carried ashore by the tides, and buried by the winds of time. Mary B probably held in her hands part of a bowl that a Chinese emperor scooped rice out of six centuries before.

We walked on, feeling like pirates on a deserted isle looking for lost booty. Mixed with the din of crashing surf and boisterous gulls, I heard baying.

"Did you hear that?" I asked.

"Hear what?"

"Sounds like a baby cow or something," I said.

Just as I said it, a stiff onshore wind blew my words away. I cocked my head in the direction of the dunes.

"It's coming from over there," I said, pointing.

"You've always had satellite dishes for ears," Mary B said, laughing.

True. My ears are quite large. We scuttled like sand crabs over a dune. On the leeward side, things were less noisy, the gulls less bullying. I heard bawling again. Then I spotted the source. Lying in the sand twenty yards away was a silver blob, shaped like an oversized rugby ball. Sand flicked from the blob's sides.

"It's a seal pup," Mary B exclaimed. "What kind of seal is it, Ranger?"

The sleek, silver-toned animal had black spots and a black nose, giving it the appearance of a Dalmatian. Coarse whiskers poked out from a long snout. The creature looked at us with shiny, coal-black eyes. Unlike the satellites on the side of my head, this pup had only holes. It was a pinniped—an earless seal. It opened its mouth and hissed at us, revealing sharp teeth. I instinctively grabbed my groin.

"It's a baby Harbor seal," I said. "I'll bet mama isn't far off either."

Female Harbor seals haul out on land to give birth, and it was rare to see a young pup alone on the beach, especially without mama around.

"We'd better get going, in case she comes back," I said.

We retraced our steps over the dunes and back to the frenzied surf zone. *What's next...a Great White shark?*

We walked along the spit, admiring an orange and black Tufted puffin bobbing in the ocean swells, just offshore. Finally, we reached the mouth of Drake's Estero. An estuary (Estero in Spanish) is where fresh water and ocean tidal waters mix, like singles during happy hour. If we accept this estuarine-singles-bar metaphor, then Drake's Estero is *the* player at the Seashore. Deriving its name from the English seafarer Sir Francis Drake, who beached his ship here four centuries earlier, the Estero is the main drainage for the Point Reyes peninsula.

I looked across to the other side, a distance of about a quarter mile. I decided I'd try to swim to the other side. *What's four hundred yards of open water, Dutton? You have a swimming merit badge, right?*

"I'm going to swim across," I told Mary B.

As I plunged in, I barely heard Mary B's rebuttal... something to do with sharks. Riverine and ocean currents immediately and simultaneously tugged and pulled at my body—one was going out, the other coming in. I turned over and freestyled, then paused to catch a breath. I'd made it only half way. I turned and faced the wide Pacific. Afternoon sun glared off undulating swells. I squinted. *Was that a dorsal fin?* Fear—the kind that makes you involuntarily piss—gripped me. I vented a warm liter of last night's Oly into the cold ocean.

#

One in every ten Great White attacks on humans worldwide occurs in what shark scientists ominously refer to as the "Red Triangle"—a section of Pacific Ocean stretching from Big Sur in northern California to Bodega Bay just north of Point Reyes. The apex of the triangle is the Farallon Islands, twenty miles offshore. I was practically swimming in a Great White country club pool, and pissing in it no less.

As I treaded water, a nightmarish scene began to unfold in my consciousness: I'm lying on the beach. Hideous, scarlet gashes crisscross my lower torso and buttocks. Bright, arterial blood spurts from a shredded leg and spills out onto the sand, creating a grotesque red and white tableau. Mary B thrusts her hands deep into my thigh, struggling to stem the red tide. They are covered in blood. But it's no use. She screams for help, but no one can hear her. Except for a lone dorsal fin slicing the surf just offshore, and mobbing gulls, we are all alone.

I turned over and swam toward shore, scissor-kicking, beating the surf with my flailing arms, sending out sonic pulses to every Carcharodon carcharias within ten miles. *Hey, some dufus who smells like piss is in the shallow end…and he swims like shit!* I reached Limantour spit, pulled myself out of the murky water, rolled onto my back and looked up at the marine sky, breathing hard. Mary B's familiar face appeared in my viewfinder.

"Are you okay?" she asked. There it was again. That tone. The one that juxtaposes concern with, "Why does he do shit like this?"

"I'm alright," I answered.

"No, you're not. You're burnt bad, Ranger." She pressed her hand to my vermillion chest, leaving a palm-shaped white pictograph.

"Let's head back. I'm hungry," I said.

A waning sun shone on a beach where only two soles—one clothed, and one not—wandered along its edge. Plovers raced in the surf. Gulls monitored our movements like drones. When we reached the dune where my clothes were piled, Mary B fetched a thick pastrami sandwich and a cold Oly from the cooler and handed both to me.

The sun had baked my skin to the second degree. Only my groin and the soles of my feet escaped blistering. We sat with our backs against a dune, watching the sun slowly drown in the ocean. A cool onshore breeze began to stir. I shivered.

"Let's get you home, Ranger."

As we packed up the Mazda, I winced with every movement. Even the worn cotton T-shirt across my back felt like steel wool.

"What a day," I said, closing the tailgate.

"Yeah, it was," Mary B seconded, "but swimming with sharks was pretty damned stupid." She shot me that look, again. Deep down, I was pretty sure it wouldn't be the last time.

#

After two days of pickling in cold bathtub water, I carefully put on my uniform and walked to work. Luckily, it was foggy. The skin on my neck and ears sloughed off like snake skin. My face was still a few shades shy of scarlet, but at least I didn't look like a boiled crustacean anymore.

I walked into the VC. Allan was manning the information desk. "You look like shit," he said. "Where have you been?"

"The beach." I reached behind my ear and made a patch of skin appear like a magician. "See?"

#

In early December, as I was nearing the end of my seasonal appointment at Point Reyes, the phone at the Bear Valley Visitor Center rang. I answered it. "Point Reyes National Seashore, can I help you?" The female voice on the other end had a distinct Dolly Parton twang to it.

"Yes, this is David Dutton."

"Yes, I'm interested."

"Yes, I understand."

"Is there housing available?"

"Yes, thank you very much."

I hung up the phone, and told Greg I needed to take an early lunch. I raced back to our trailer. Mary B was outside filling birdfeeders.

"Mammoth Cave just called," I said, out of breath. Her eyes grew wide.

"Really?" The word ended on a high octave.

"Yeah, really. It's a permanent Park Ranger Interpreter job. They want me there before Christmas. What should I tell them?"

Mary B dropped the sack of sunflower seed, walked over and hugged me tightly.

"I'll take that as a yes."

She smiled, and nodded.

A fish has finally risen, Ranger Dutton!

Kentucky Bound and Won't Slow Down for Dead Raccoons or Joggers!

Lately it occurs to me what a long, strange trip it's been.
~ Grateful Dead, Truckin'

It is approximately 2,357 miles from Point Reyes National Seashore to Mammoth Cave National Park, not including the 5.8 mile detour to Inverness to pick up some frozen It's-It's. It would be a long ride.

In mid-December, after calling the seashore our home for seven months, we emptied the sand from our shoes and said goodbye to Banana slugs, Acorn woodpeckers, Morgan horses, blackberries, apples, Great White sharks, drippy fog and our singlewide trailer. We left the Marin Headlands, bound for Monterey, the first stop on our cross-country journey. On the other side of the Golden Gate Bridge, we merged with zillions of other crazed California drivers, most, hell-bent on getting to their destination before everyone else.

We exited the rakish environs of US 101, and entered the more laggard surroundings of Castroville. Fields of spiky artichoke plants laid out in long straight rows bordered either side of the road. Soon, we skirted the deserted Fort Ord rifle ranges bordering Hwy 1 (*...I wish all the ladies...*) and by late afternoon reached Mary B's house on Cimarron Street in Monterey. We pulled to the curb. The front door opened. An immense dog raced across the front lawn, and bowled Mary B flat.

"Daniel," she cried out.

Daniel was a 125-pound black-and-tan German shepherd with a weakness for cherry-flavored gourmet jellybeans. He was, and still is, the most magnificent dog I've ever known. Mary B had raised him since he could fit in her palm. He was her child, and by law, my adopted son. When Mary B and I were dating, I'd play fetch with Daniel, tossing tree branches into the Carmel River. Daniel would swim out and retrieve them, like they were matchsticks. When he grew tired of the game, he'd wrap his formidable jaws around the branch I was attempting to throw, and sit. Game over.

Daniel would be making the long trip to Kentucky with us. Finding space enough for him in the back of the Mazda would be a packing challenge though. We rented a 4 x6 U-Haul, and Mary's father bought us a camper shell for the Mazda. Over the next two days, Daniel never left Mary B's side as she sorted out her life; what to pack, what to leave behind. We were leaving the state that'd been the backdrop for our entire lives, and were bound for a state neither of us had ever seen. There were no guarantees we'd be coming back. But duty called. If I wanted to become a permanent Park Ranger with the National Park Service—then it would have to start in Kentucky.

On the morning of our departure, Daniel hopped into the back of the Mazda and sat. After a round of handshakes, hugs and tears, Mary B and I hopped into the Mazda too, and waved goodbye. We pushed away from the curb, and charted a course for the San Joaquin Valley and the Tehachapi Mountains. Beyond, lay the Mojave Desert, the Basin and Range country of the Southwest, the great plains of the heartland, Old Man River, the land of Davy Crockett, and finally, the limestone caverns of Mammoth Cave.

Over the next five days, we traveled through eight states. Daniel left his scent in every one of them. He was especially generous in Texas, leaving calling cards at every gas station and rest stop across the Panhandle. Maybe the Moo Shu pork we had for lunch in Tucumcari didn't agree with him.

Road Axiom #1: Never order Chinese takeout from a restaurant that looks like a converted Exxon station.

Despite our best efforts at sanitation, by the time we reached West Memphis, Arkansas, our lunar module was a repository of road effluvia. Stowaway corn nuts, colorful M & M's, soiled napkins, paper straws, sticky foil wrappers, dried French fries, gutted Heinz ketchup packets, receipts, maps, combs, crumbs, coins, and coffee-stained Styrofoam cups all found niches in our cramped cab. Worse still, the Mazda's "new car" smell abandoned us somewhere outside Oklahoma City.

Late on day five, we exited I-65 at Park City, Kentucky, a community on the fringe of Mammoth Cave National Park. The town had five hundred residents on a good day, one stoplight, a bank, a hardware store with a porch and wooden benches, a furniture shop, a post office, a corner grocery and a railroad crossing. It also had a phone booth.

Before leaving Point Reyes, one of the clerks at Mammoth Cave hooked me up with a Park City landlord. I pulled into the driveway of a two bedroom, brick and wood structure on East 3rd Street. A gargantuan maple tree stood in the front yard. Yellow leaves drooped from its thick branches. I climbed out of the cab, wiped away Fig Newton crumbs, and stretched. Mary B went around to the back of the Mazda and let out Daniel, who wasted no time christening the maple tree, the front porch, and everything else on the grounds, even after his spigot dried up.

The three of us stood on the front lawn, exhausted and excited at the same time. This would be our new home. The sun had disappeared, and cold winter shadows filled in the landscape. Twenty nine cups of road java were ringing up my switchboard. I walked around back and placed a long distance call. Buttoning up, I found the house key under the mat on the back porch, in accordance with the plan. *So far, so good.*

The interior of the house was cold and dark, and smelled like new linoleum in a musty warehouse. I groped along the wall until I found a light switch, and flipped it. Nothing. The utilities hadn't been turned on yet. *Not so good.* I walked around to the front of the house, where Daniel had just treed his first Kentucky squirrel.

"Well," I said to Mary B, "I'll need my uniform tomorrow. Why don't we just unload some of the stuff into the house, check into a hotel, and come back tomorrow?" And thus, did the unloading process start. We carried cardboard boxes across the lawn, up the front porch steps, and into a dark house.

I'd finally managed to see the back wall of the U-haul trailer (never pack the things you'll need first in the very back of the load), when Daniel's Rin Tin Tin bark backed me out of it. *What's that, boy? Mary B has fallen off the front porch and has a severe, medial malleolous fracture of her right ankle? No way!* Daniel looked at me pleadingly with amber eyes, then ran toward the front of the house, barking as he went. Mary B was on her back with her feet up in the air, like a flipped-over Box turtle on the side of the road. Daniel nuzzled his mistress. I knelt down.

"Are you okay?" *Damned stupid question, Dutton. Of course she isn't.* Shock had already sent her a shivering greeting card.

"I fell off the porch," she said, then added the words that straightened the hairs on my nape, "I heard a snap."

I helped her to her feet, and we hobbled a short distance to the truck. Under Daniel's watchful eye, I placed her into the Mazda, ran around to the driver's side, and cranked up the heater. Mary B needed to get to a hospital, fast. *But where the hell is one?*

The porch light of the house across the street glowed brightly. I walked over and knocked on the front door. An older man in a heavy flannel shirt peeled back the front door. Cooped-up heat rushed from the house and hugged me.

"Sir, we're moving into the house across the street," I began, surprised at the timidity in my voice. *You're supposed to be the white knight here, Dutton. Quit sounding like a Girl Scout selling cookies.* The man looked over my shoulder at the idling Mazda in the driveway across the street, then turned a stern gaze on me. He started with my sneakers, and ended with my eyes, which, I'm sure, were bloodshot from miles of interstate driving.

"My wife fell and broke her ankle," I continued. "Can you tell me how to get to a hospital?"

"I'm Frankie Toms," the man finally said. *Wow, a voice straight out of Gone with the Wind.* He stuck out a large, bony hand. I shook it. His grip was vise-like. "That's Tommie Duvall's place," he said.

I'd never heard such an accent. Ever. He spoke slowly. I felt as though I could tie both my shoes before he got his next sentence out.

"Yes, sir. We're renting it. I'm a Park Ranger at the Cave." I tried sounding colloquial, referring to the longest cave system in the world as "the cave." Mr. Toms smiled.

"Well then, you must knows Tommie's bigger brother, Joe. He does guidin' out there. Mostlys in the summer, cause he teaches school." School came out *skoo*.

Shivering on Frankie Tom's front porch that icy December night, I discovered a truism about Kentuckians, and Southerners in general—pleasantries *always* come before business.

"No sir, I'm afraid not. Tomorrow will be my first day," I said.

"I'm sure you will meet 'em, sooner—"

"I really need to get my wife to a hospital, Mr. Toms. Is there one nearby?"

My abruptness caused him to furrow his eyebrows a bit, but I didn't care. Mary needed help.

"Why yes, there's a hospital in Glasgow."

"Good. Can you give me directions?"

For the next several minutes, I listened to my soon-to-be neighbor's directions. I tried to make mental asterisks whenever he referenced navigational landmarks like, "Turn right at the next blacktop road," or "Veer left at the house with the tractor in the yard," and "If you pass a large sorghum field, you's gone too far." Mostly though, I just listened to how he talked. When he'd finished, I shook his hand again, and sprinted back to Mary B and Daniel. She was in awful pain. Daniel rested his massive head on her shoulder.

"Do you know where the hospital is, Ranger?"

I looked right at her. "Yes," I lied.

#

I backed out of the driveway, and turned onto a two lane highway. It was cold enough to snow. Silhouettes of farm fences and rows of dented mailboxes sitting catawampus on dilapidated wooded posts materialized in my high beams. I looked for the landmarks that Frankie Toms mentioned—the house with the tractor in the yard, sorghum fields—but they, along with everything else, were swallowed whole by the inky Kentucky night. *Might as well be navigating with a sextant!* I turned right onto a paved road (blacktop road?). It segued into another, wider, asphalt road. Mary B moaned. A green and white highway sign with the word "Glasgow" poked out of a hedgerow. *Hadn't Mr. Toms mentioned Glasgow in his directions?* I drove on, relieved to see twinkling icons of civilization in the distance.

"Kind of looks like a hospital up there," Mary B said, hoping.

I turned off the main drag, and into a parking lot that fronted a large, red, brick building. I got out and rushed inside. Glass doors sluiced open. On the other side, men and women in saggy bathrobes and fuzzy slippers shuffled slowly on a floor they could see their reflections in. Elevator music cooed from ceiling speakers. In the corner of the room, seniors in wheelchairs nodded sleepily in front of a TV. Urine, and its close cousin, bleach, loitered about in the shiny corridors. *This isn't the ER.* I spotted the reception desk and walked over to it. A middle-aged woman put down her magazine, and braced for my landing.

"Can I help you?" she asked. You came out *yew*.

"Yes, ma'am. I'm looking for the hospital. I thought this was it." The woman stifled a laugh.

"This is the convalescent hospital. The real hospital's jus' down the road."

"How do I get to it?"

Unlike Mr. Toms, the woman's directions omitted references to farm equipment or sorghum fields. Five minutes later, Mary B sat on a cold examination table with her bloated, disfigured ankle on full display. A doctor in a crisp white lab coat and a stethoscope necktie pulled back the curtain divider. A perky young nurse shadowed him. The doctor walked around the table, cocking his head this way and that, and began palpating Mary B's foot. She winced and shifted her weight, like she was sitting on roofing tacks. When the doctor finally spoke, it was in a staccato, Indian dialect. He turned and spoke to the nurse. Mary B and I looked at each other. I tried to understand what the Indian doctor and the Kentucky nurse were talking about, but it was as if their words were in a cement mixer. "Fractured" and "joint instability" rolled down the chute, along with a viscous mix of consonants and syllables, most of which were indecipherable. After a few minutes, they left, pulling the curtain behind them.

"What did they say?" Mary B asked.

"I haven't a clue."

I stared at Mary B's purplish ankle. Her swollen toes stuck out like rigid cow udders. I laughed out loud at the absurdity of our predicament.

"How the hell did we end up in a hospital in the middle of a sorghum field in Kentucky?"

Mary B managed a weak laugh. The doctor and the twenty-something nurse entered the examining room again. The doctor carried a splint and some gauze. He carefully placed the splint under Mary B's ankle and began wrapping. As he did, the preppy nurse spoke up.

"I sprained my ankle once, cheerleading in high*skoo*," she said. "It ain't never been right since." Mary B rolled her eyes.

Medical Axiom #1: If you're a medical professional, never comment on how much shittier a patient's injuries can get.

Three hours later, Mary B was asleep in our hotel room. The pain meds had worked their magic. Her right leg was in a plaster cast, propped up on stacked pillows. From her knee down, it resembled a huge, white capital L. Daniel laid his head on her chest, awake and on guard. *Has there ever been a dog more loyal?*

I went into the bathroom, and stared at my grizzled pelage. I needed to shave my Point Reyes beard. Mammoth Cave Park Rangers were allowed mustaches but not beards. Just another adjustment I'd have to make.

I'd meant to buy shaving supplies, but the evening's events kyboshed that. The nice lady at the front desk let me borrow her daughter's blunt-nosed scissors—the kind first graders use to cut out paper snowflakes with. I pulled and cut with the kiddy scissors, then rummaged in the bathroom until I found one of Mary B's road-weary Bic shavers.

When I finished shaving, shredded bits of toilet paper with bloody dots stuck to my chin and cheeks. I walked into the bedroom and quietly pulled my wrinkled uniform and Smokey-the-Bear hat from a cardboard box—the same box I was retrieving when Mary B fell from grace. I hung up the uniform, placed Smokey on the dresser, and peeled back the covers. I closed my eyes, but sleep was another interstate further. Tomorrow I would report to work as a permanent, fulltime, Park Ranger with the National Park Service. Great. It's what I dreamed about. At the moment, though, what I really wanted was a tall glass of Kentucky bourbon.

The Lowly Snake

Indiana Jones: There's a big snake in the plane, Jock!
Jock: Oh, that's just my pet snake Reggie.
Indiana Jones: I hate snakes, Jock! I hate 'em!
Jock: C'mon, show a little backbone, will ya!
~ Indiana Jones, Raiders of the Lost Ark

Mary B, Daniel and I, arrived at Mammoth Cave National Park, about a week before Christmas, 1983. We spent the holiday in our tiny house on East 3rd Street in Park City, huddled around an aging floor furnace. Mary B hobbled about in her cast with a thick sock over her exposed toes. Everywhere she went, Daniel followed. Kentucky experienced record cold in the winter of 1983-1984. Often, we awoke in the mornings to inches of accumulated ice on the inside of our kitchen window. When nighttime temps dipped to a gelid minus twenty degrees, I placed an old army blanket over the Mazda's engine to keep it warm. It seemed to do the trick. The Mazda always cranked up in the mornings, much to the chagrin of Mr. Tom's, whose Chevy truck needed infusions of jumper cable sauce to get going.

A bitter cold winter morphed into an unusually wet spring. So much rain fell over central Kentucky and washed into Mammoth Cave's porous limestone, that it flooded the cave, causing cancellations of the very popular Echo River Tour, which featured a flat bottom boat ride. As violent spring tornadoes ripped the surface and rain wreaked havoc on the subterranean, Mary B and I wondered aloud, "What have we got ourselves into?"

Summer arrived, and with it, vapors thicker than taffy. The Chief of Interpretation assigned me to do "surface walks." Anywhere else in the NPS they'd be called "nature walks." While my colleagues worked in the cool 55 degree chill below ground, I basked in triple digit temperatures above it. Although Mammoth Cave National Park (MACA in NPS parlance) is renowned for its underground secrets, I quickly discovered that Mammoths' surface world held secrets of its own. For a California kid growing up hiking the legendary granite spires of the Sierra Nevada Mountains, sifting through an Eastern deciduous forest, with its closed leaf canopy, was an altogether different experience. I became acquainted with some of the park's lesser seen wildlife— poisonous snakes, blood-sucking ticks, and pernicious chiggers.

Chiggers are the larvae of mites. They loiter around vegetation like teenagers outside a liquor store. When an unsuspecting host passes by, they latch onto it and insert feeding structures, injecting enzymes that destroy flesh. Then they suck their fill—a kind of tissue milkshake—and drop off satiated, smoking a cigarette. The process leaves an itchy welt. I found this out the hard way trudging through waist-high grass, while attempting to catch a bullfrog one afternoon. What I caught instead was the attention of hundreds of parched chiggers. I'm sure the tiny, parasitic bastards snickered when they saw me coming. "Hey y'all, here comes that dufus from California. Dig in!"

The next morning I awoke with hundreds and hundreds of bites covering my legs, waist and scrotum. I looked like a swollen rash with protruding legs. I scratched with a fury— tearing at the pimply-looking welts—until they oozed blood. After work, I'd speed home to Park City, shifting and scratching, pour a cold bath and plunge in. Cold water was like a narcotic, only it came from the tap and not from some guy in a trenchcoat on the corner.

Scratching in public became problematic. It might be acceptable to scratch your scrotum in full view of everybody if you are a major league pitcher or a construction worker, but certainly not if you wear the uniform of a National Park Service Ranger. Whenever I thought no one was watching, I'd sneak behind a tree and scratch like a dog with fleas, only to look up and see a family staring at me with my hands down my pants. During our weekly grocery outings to Bowling Green, I'd steal handfuls of ice from the produce section, and slather my red-dotted legs.

"Chigger bites," I'd say to a gawking produce clerk.

I should've felt good knowing that my protein helped larval chiggers achieve the arachnid equivalent of puberty. Instead, I felt used and dirty.

#

As autumn began edging out a stubbornly hot Kentucky summer, my chigger woes tapered off. The frenzied staccato of summer's chirping crickets gradually faded. Male crickets gave up trying to attract mates, succumbing to the advancing cold. Of course, there were still a few diehards, trying for a late season score, or as my southern brethren put it, "He's just tryin' to get 'em some."

Throughout the park, oaks, poplars, sweet gums, beeches, and maples erupted in a cavalcade of colors. Having been cloaked in boring, green chlorophyll for most of the year, they were now free to strut in riotous shades of red, gold, plum and yellow. It was the leaf pageant they'd waited patiently for all year, and they made the most of it. As fall advanced, creatures above land and below, punched their circadian time clocks, and settled in for a long winter shift. They wouldn't clock out until the Spring Equinox.

And so, on a cool, late September evening, I gave my last campfire program of the season. I called my presentation "Their Blood Runs Cold." I shamelessly appropriated it from a book of the same name, by noted herpetologist Dr. Whitfield Gibbons. Mary B designed a colorful snaky poster, which was displayed in the VC lobby on Saturdays to help promote the program.

I arrived at the amphitheater early, and set about making a fire, building it teepee style, using dry, oak logs. Visitors wandered in and chose their seats, like bears at a salmon run. Mary B sat in the front row with Daniel. I sat down next to them, anxiously tapping my boot. Mary B put a hand on my knee, and smiled. She always knew when I was antsy. Daniel squatted with his haunches on the bench and his front paws on the ground. When it was time, I walked over to the fire-pit, and struck a match. Smoke spiraled straight up in the cool evening air, as if being pulled by an invisible wire. I climbed the steps to the stage, switched on the microphone, and began my shtick. The Kodak carousel behind the screen whirred to life and advanced my first slide. The campfire spat embers, sending fiery tendrils skyward. Everything was going well. As I advanced through my first few slides, I kept hearing a woman's voice in the front row. At first, I tried to ignore it. Several hundred people were dialed into what I was saying, and I needed to be focused. But the voice wouldn't go away. It grew more insistent. By the third slide, the woman's voice whispered hoarsely, like an offstage dialogue coach giving lines to a forgetful actor.

"Ranger, there's a copperhead down here!" Mary B said.

I stopped in mid sentence, and looked down. She gripped Daniel's collar firmly. His ears were pinned back, and his upper lip had a nasty curl to it. Then I saw what he saw—a large Northern copperhead snake, possibly a yard long, undulating in the direction of the low benches, where the audience sat, blissfully unaware. Although it was poisonous, and posed a serious threat, all I kept thinking was "hibernaculum"—an underground hangout that copperheads use to overwinter. *Maybe he's on his way to a sleepover?* Another look and it was clear this snake didn't have ZZZs on his mind. He was fully aroused and on the prowl. I swallowed hard and made a pronouncement.

"Folks, we have a poisonous snake up front."

There were gasps and some muted screams. People lifted their feet like the ground below them was suddenly molten lava. Someone shouted "Please don't kill the snake!" I remember thinking: *Park Rangers don't indiscriminately kill wildlife.* Except for chiggers. To them, I'm a serial killer.

I rushed inside the amphitheater looking for the snake stick—a broom handle with a coat hanger duct taped to the end of it. When I came back out, a crowd had gathered around the coiled serpent. I waded in, and worked the hook under the pit viper's massive body. The circle widened. Using both hands, I hoisted the copperhead, and walked slowly to a stone retaining wall adjacent to the amphitheater. The copperhead swiveled its large head and looked directly at me. *Stay put big fella.* I placed him on the other side of the wall, and watched as he disappeared seamlessly into the leaf litter. Then I hurried back to the amphitheater, put the snake stick away, and cued the next slide. An image of a copperhead with a three foot vertical pupil appeared on the large silver screen. A hush settled over the crowd.

I had their undivided attention.

#

After my last campfire program of the season, the weather turned noticeably colder. Jack-o-lanterns gave way to Jack Frost. *Auld Lang Syne* grudgingly gave way to Spring Equinox and rejuvenation. Growing up in California, I hadn't much appreciation for spring, having suffered miserably from allergies when the grasses that felted the foothills came of age and spread their seeds. Then, when they became brittle and a fire hazard in the summer heat, dad tasked his sons with chopping them down.

Things were different in Kentucky though. I began to appreciate the words of poets like e.e. Cummings, Robert Burns and D. H. Lawrence, when they wrote about the zest and rebirth of spring. I'd never experienced the full spectrum of green, until I saw Kentucky redbuds, poplars, oaks, hickories and beeches, unfurl their foliage. Sugars surged up their cambiums and nourished their sprouting leaves. And from there, it was an easy leap to chlorophyll addiction.

Animals, too, took advantage of the warming spring sun, crawling or slithering from their winter lairs. Box turtles with half dome carapaces, roamed the woods hoping to snatch pudgy night crawlers flushed out by spring rains. The croaked choruses of Spring peepers shrilled from woodland puddles, their joyous song amounting to a seasonal toggle switch—winter off, spring on. Birds with plumages rivaling a Sherwin Williams catalog flitted about in newly minted trees. Male feathered virtuosos—their testes having swelled to an unbelievable 300 times their normal size—twittered from every imaginable perch...*Hey baby, over here!*

And so, on a glorious spring day, Mary B, Daniel, and I went for a drive. Daniel poked his furry head into the cab, keeping a watchful eye on my shifting. The backroad slalomed in and out of hollers, and soon we came across a dark tree branch, as thick as a pool cue, lying unassumingly in the road. I skirted around it.

"That's a snake!" Mary B said.

"No way."

I pulled to the shoulder, and walked over to have a closer look. Sure enough, a snake lay stretched out on the asphalt without a care in the world. I don't know what it is about snakes and roads, but they go together like a drunk and a double-malt Scotch. Nothing good ever comes from it.

"You're damn lucky you don't have Michelin marks running across your skinny spine," I said to the earless reptile.

The serpent had a wide head and keeled scales, and a peculiar bent-up nose, like a car hood that'd been in a head-on collision. It flattened its head and hissed, then feigned a strike, like a boxer flicking a jab. I backed away and took a knee, watching as it sucked in air then let it out forcibly. I'd never seen a snake behave like this. I approached cautiously and grabbed the ruler-length snake behind the head. It writhed and opened its jaws wide. I looked in. No fangs. Mary B got out of the truck, came over and looked down the snake's throat, like a doctor examining a patient's tonsils.

"It's got fangs. See, in the very back."

"What?"

I peered in again. Sure enough there were two tiny curved teeth. *I'm holding a rear-fanged snake!*

Mary B laughed. "What are you going to do now, Ranger?"

"Hell if I know."

"Why don't you just let it go?"

We walked over to the side of the road, and I gently tossed the snake into a shallow ditch. Lickety-split, it flipped over, convulsed violently like it had too much cheap tequila, and went limp. That was it. The snake was dead. I couldn't believe it. We turned to go back to the truck, and just when I was thinking I'd caused its demise, the snake righted itself and started to slink off. It's hard not to be anthropomorphic about these sorts of things—perhaps too many Disney movies while growing up—but I definitely detected an "Oh shit" expression on the snake's scaly face.

The serpent turned belly up again, and went through the same set of behaviors—convulsing, gagging, agony, the whole spiel. The snake's routine was a ruse of course, a clever defense mechanism designed to trick predators into thinking it was dead. It might have worked too, except that he forgot to *stay* dead. I walked back to the truck and grabbed a pillowcase, which I kept for occasions like these. Halfway through the snake's second act of "I'm absolutely dead this time," I stuffed him into it.

We took the little snake back home with us. I constructed a wire and plywood cage, adding the requisite décor—rocks, sand, sticks, mayonnaise jar lid with water. The cage needed to be sturdy enough to protect the snake from thuggish raccoons that roamed the park nightly, violating trash cans and shaking down frightened campers for Twinkies.

Our little Thespian turned out to be an Eastern hognose snake (*Heterodon platyrhinos*), a nonpoisonous species. The Latin genus to which the snake belongs literally means "different tooth," a clear reference to the curved teeth in the back of their mouth. The hissing and convulsing we'd witnessed was meant to convey badassness. As a result, the harmless hognose has earned some pretty wicked monikers—spearhead, puff adder, hissing sand snake, and my favorite—blow viper.

Hognose snakes primarily feed on toads. Toads know this, so they make themselves huge by inflating air sacs along the sides of their bodies through respiration. Turns out, if you're a toad, having a beachball physique comes in handy when someone is trying to swallow you.

Toads and hognose snakes have coexisted on earth for nearly 190 million years. Over the millennia, The Great Snake Council convened many times to figure out a solution to the conundrum of swallowing toads. Countless committees and subcommittees were formed. Workshops, symposiums and endless roundtables were devoted to the subject. White papers were even written, although with no hands, it must've been difficult.

Finally, a snake from the house of *Heterodon* rose to champion an amazingly simple idea: Why not grow teeth capable of piercing the toad's air sac defenses? The motion was unanimously adopted, and that is why today, hognose snakes possess sharp, curved teeth so that they can spear the toad's air sacs and swallow their deflated prey. But the toads, not to be outdone, developed another defense mechanism, even niftier than their beachball trick. If a predator tries to make a Toad McNugget out of them, they can secrete poison from a pair of glands called parotid glands, which are located just behind their head. The secreted poison is reputed to be worse than warm Schlitz. The predator spits out the horribly tasting toad, and runs off looking for a drinking fountain. Apparently though, hognose snakes aren't bothered by warm Schlitz.

I was never sure what sex our hognose was. The only surefire way to find out is to probe the cloaca—a common opening, hidden under scale the snake uses to poop, pee and reproduce. Although both sexes possess a cloaca, male hognose snakes have a hemipenis, which is forked, and also grooved to allow semen to flow into the female's cloaca. Fortunately, in hognose species, males have a more obvious gender distinction—longer and thicker tails than females. Turns out our little tree branch had a budding sapling all his own. He was a guy. That came as a relief. There just wasn't enough sour mash in all of Kentucky to entice me to go cloaca probing.

We named the hognose Pig, because he ate like one. One night, I dropped three plump toads into his cage, and like a reptilian David Copperfield, Pig disappeared them all. Once, I even tossed a toad into Pig's cage the size of a billiard ball. It was a MACA death match: Bufo "The 8-Ball" Toad vs. Pig "The Hose" Hognose. Pig's cage sat just outside our bedroom window, and all through the night I kept hearing muffled slams. The next morning I peeked into Pig's cage. His jaws were wrapped around the globular amphibian, tenaciously hanging on, getting knocked silly every time the toad hopped this way or that. After work, I checked on Pig again. Through sheer tenacity, he'd managed to swallow something four times his own body width. He had a scaly, shit-eating grin on his face, like Jack Nicholson courtside at a Lakers game.

Finding toads for Pig proved easier than I'd imagined. On balmy spring nights, Mary B and I grabbed flashlights and pillowcases, and went looking. We had with us a secret weapon—a chow mutt, Kentucky-bred toad snifter. We "acquired" him when we lived in Park City the winter before. Acquire is too polite a term, I suppose. When the little shit neighbor kids began hurling darts at the dog, we kidnapped him, and never asked for ransom. His fur was the color of cinnamon, although I argued his fur color more resembled lightly toasted marshmallows. But naming a dog "Marshmallows" just wouldn't do, especially in the south. So when we moved into park housing the following spring, Cinnamon came along too.

Whenever Cinnamon spotted a toad, his tail stiffened like a pointer. One evening after a rainstorm, he made the mistake of trying to eat a lopping toad (Remember the warm Schlitz?). He ran back to us, frothing like he'd just swallowed a bar of Dial. He shook his head, jettisoning slimy foam all over us. After that, he just located the toads, content to let us do the bagging.

Hognose snakes have been known to cycle through the same set of behaviors—flipping over, convulsing, and coughing up their tongue, going limp—many times consecutively. *But how many times?* I decided to find out. One summer afternoon, I placed Pig on the lawn, and sat down on the front porch steps, clipboard in hand. A wayward chigger crept across my notepad, and I smashed it with my thumb. When I approached Pig, he immediately morphed into his convulsing, hissing tirade with Shakespearean gusto. I studiously recorded a hash mark on the clipboard, and righted him again. Every time I did, Pig rifled through his bag of tricks, invariably ending in listlessness. I'd recorded thirty-seven hash marks (and a red spot from the smashed chigger), when on the thirty-eighth try, Pig didn't budge. He looked up at me like John McEnroe questioning an umpire's call at Wimbledon... *You can't be serious?* Apparently, it takes thirty-eight tries before a hognose snake just says, "The hell with it!"

#

Throughout the spring and summer, Pig slithered his way into our lives, and our shoes, and our pantry, and our couch, and our shower. He grew steadily bigger, thanks to a metric ton of toad meat. Every few weeks he'd push out of his skin. Snakes have to shed. As they grow, their skin does not. Picture a teenager trying to fit into a pair of footie pajamas.

On Friday nights, Pig coiled up in Mary B's lap as we watched a sockless Don Johnson and his suave partner, Detective "Rico" Tubbs, bust Colombian drug lords in *Miami Vice*. Pig never blinked, even when the commercials came on. Not having eyelids probably had something to do with it. On Saturday nights he was the star attraction during my campfire programs. Kids loved his *I'm going to die* antics, and watched in awe as he flipped upside down and stuck out his tongue. I always rewarded Pig with a toad when we got home.

One summer morning while I was underground, Pig lay stretched out on the windowsill over the kitchen sink, doing what he liked best—basking in the morning sun. Mary B had just finished the breakfast dishes when the telephone repairman pulled into our driveway. She greeted him at the front door, and showed him the rotary telephone on the wall in our kitchen. Pig ignored the Rastafarian repairman with his clangy tool belt and long dreadlocks. The technician however, did not ignore Pig.

"Mon, you have snake!" he shouted, backpedaling out the door.

Mary B plucked Pig from his perch, and put him in his cage outside. When she entered the house, the repairman was speedily stripping candy-cane colored wires, all the time looking over his shoulder. When he'd finished, he collected his tools, raced to his truck, and sped off. Over dinner that night, Mary B mused that the guy worked so fast, it was a miracle his dreadlocks and telephone wires didn't somehow get woven together.

By the time that Pig and I did our last campfire program, autumn was a whisker away. Leaves murmured amongst themselves in the cool breezes, making plans for the kaleidoscopic fall leaf pageant. Wood smoke hung like fog in the hollers again. Crickets chirped less. It was time to let Pig go. He needed time to find a suitable place to overwinter. While in captivity (using the term loosely here, given he had the run of the house), Pig had quadrupled in length to nearly four feet, and had doubled in girth. The once puny reptile was now an Atlas of a snake. No more would toads kick sand in his face.

On a brilliant October afternoon, we loaded up the Mazda, and charted a course for the spot where Pig first fooled us with his mimicry a half-year before. Mary B stroked Pig's wide head as he lay contentedly in her lap. Daniel stretched out in the truck bed, soaking up autumn rays pouring through the camper shell's portal windows. Soon, we reached the ditch where it all began. A barbed-wire fence suspended by hardwood saplings separated the ditch from a field of yellow, crinkly grass.

Mary B knelt down and released Pig, and he immediately stretched out in the bright sun. Suddenly, I heard the distinctive cry of a Red-tailed hawk, and cast a worried glance skyward.

A mature raptor spiraled overhead, his cinnabar tail fanning out like a Japanese parasol. He probably eyed Pig lying in the grass, and had already dialed up an aerial strike. An ugly image flashed in my head: Pig writhing helplessly in steely talons as the raptor flew to a far-off branch to eviscerate its still live prey, glottis to cloaca.

When I looked back, Pig's thick tail was slowly disappearing under a hedgerow. *He's safe.* Mary B and I turned and walked back to the truck. I was going to miss Pig. He'd brought so much unexpected joy into our lives.

"Stay off the roads," I said, like a father cautioning his teenage son to not drink and drive.

"What did you say?" Mary B asked.

"Nothing."

We climbed back into the Mazda. The fall sun was intense. I flipped down the visor.

"Goodbye Pig," Mary B said, wistfully.

I pulled onto the road, mindful of any tree branches lying about.

Beyond the Call of Duty

*How long a minute is depends on what side
of the bathroom door you're on.*
~ Author unknown

By the summer of 1986, I'd been leading people into and out of the longest cave in the world for two and a half years, and was proud of my perfect record—zero visitors lost. Interpretive Park Rangers at Mammoth Cave National Park called themselves guides. We stood behind a half-moon desk in the Visitor Center, our shoes highly buffed, our uniform creases knife-edged, dispensing information to throngs of visitors.

Families milled about in the spacious VC lobby, pacing anxiously over thread-bare carpet, waiting for their turn to be taken underground. They looked at exhibits which were shiny and new during the Kennedy administration. In the corner of the VC, a young mother sat on a bench breastfeeding her baby. This was good. A fussy infant could torpedo a cave tour.

Whereas many guides found desk duty to be tedious, I found it to be fun. In addition to answering the ubiquitous question, "Where are the bathrooms?" 1,039 times before 9:00 AM coffee break, I'd give seriously nuanced responses to questions such as "What time is the ten o'clock Historic Cave tour?" or "How much of the cave is underground?" The information desk was the first echelon for visitors, and the public expected to see a smiling, polite, informative Park Ranger.

As guides, we very often were called upon to referee family spats over which cave tour to take. "Grandma can walk four miles in the cave. Yeah. Let's take the Half-Day tour!" *Really, kid?*

"Well, her cane looks kinda wore out," I'd say. "Maybe try this tour instead."

Sadly, I often had long conversations with grandfathers and grandmothers that stayed behind while the rest of the family ventured underground.

Once a tour was decided upon, I'd direct visitors to the ticket sales area in the rear of the building, where they purchased cave tickets, sometimes from another smiling, polite, informative Park Ranger—Mary B.

When we first moved into the Park in the spring of 1984, Mary B got a job at Mammoth Cave Concessions—a conclave of gift shops that schlocked Mammoth Cave shot glasses and postcards from the 1950's showing Park Rangers in the cave, wearing full length, stiffly-buttoned coats. Later, she applied for a Park Ranger position, selling tickets for cave tours. I have to admit, Mary B looked cute in her Smokey-the-bear hat. I'd have bought a cave ticket from her.

A large group waited in the breezeway between the administration building and the VC, for the first tour of the day—the Historic Cave Tour. A guide with an insanely long maglite lassoed to his uniform belt talked to them. The tour was a cross-section of Americana: in the rear were young lovers hoping for some dark cave nooky; in the front were senior citizens, straining to hear, wishing they didn't have that second cup of coffee; and in the middle, were parents with small children in tow—moms carrying sweaters, dads fiddling with camcorders.

With my morning stint at the information desk up, I went through a side door, and descended steep stairs into the basement, where the Guide Lounge was located. The word "lounge" conjures images of elegantly dressed women clinking cocktail glasses, men in tuxedos smoking Havanas, and possibly a roulette wheel.

Our lounge—a cockroach-infested hovel with décor leftover from the 1960s—consisted of ass-worn armchairs, saggy couches, a smelly bathroom and a funky linoleum lunch table with wobbly chrome legs. But it was *our* hovel. A watering hole where we could bitch, enjoy a cold Coke, tell off-color jokes or sing spirituals. Oh yes, those homegrown Kentucky guides could belt out such a heartfelt rendition of "The Old Rugged Cross," it'd put a tear in your eye.

On this morning the guide lounge was its usual frenetic whirl. Guides shined their shoes as if they were going to Sunday school. Another busied himself sewing a button on his 1800's costume pants he'd wear for the Lantern Tour—an excursion into the cave with only kerosene lanterns to light the way. The Wild Cave guides checked batteries and headlamps for their spelunking trek. Others twisted torches made from brown, Fruit-of-the Loom underwear scraps. Later, they'd be soaked in kerosene, hung from the end of a hickory torch stick, set on fire, and flung into remote crevices of the cave to recreate how guides showcased Mammoth Cave in the 19th century. I could fling torches with the accuracy of Joe Montana, but when it came to rolling them…well, I sucked.

In the corner of the lounge, several seasoned guides were recounting the heroic exploits of a former cave guide they called Scoop Drennan. It sounded interesting, so I pulled up a chair, grabbed a tin of shoe polish, and listened in. Apparently, Ranger Drennan was trailing a tour one day when a visitor desperately needed to go number two. There were no restrooms in the part of the cave they were in, so quick thinking Scoop grabbed a plastic trash can liner.

According to the story, Scoop held the liner as the man squatted, then carried the bag of shit the rest of the way out of the cave, thereby completing the crappiest trifecta in the history of Mammoth Cave. I'd heard stories of cave guides doing extraordinary things—delivering babies, performing CPR—but carrying someone's crap out of the cave? *Man, the Park Service doesn't pay me enough to do that.* I started to rise out of my chair, but a strong hand on my shoulder kept me there.

"Hey Dutton, looks like you and me are doin' the Half Day."

I looked up into the eyes of Chet "Boom-Boom" Giles—a guide who suffered from macular degeneration. It's not clear how Chet got his nickname, although the moniker was apt. He enjoyed zooming up and down quiet back roads of Kentucky's Bluegrass Country on his Harley, terrorizing the local livestock. Even though the state of Kentucky probably considered him legally blind, Boom-Boom could spot a bat on a cave wall fifty feet away. I could eat a metric ton of carrots and still not make that claim!

The Half Day tour was physically challenging. Not as much as the Wild Cave tour—a spelunking adventure characterized by wasp-waisted passages with names like the birth canal or mole hole—but strenuous nonetheless. One of the highlights of the tour was having lunch in the Snowball Dining Room, 267 feet underground. This spacious cavern once sported ornate gypsum formations that looked like shaved snow cones. In the decades following the park's establishment in 1941, smoking was allowed in the cave. Tobacco (Kentuckians call it burley), is the state's number one *legal* cash crop. The refulgent gypsum formations were like virgin lung tissue to the tobacco smoke. Picture a metropolitan city a day or two after a major snowstorm; sooty, blackened snow piled high on sidewalks and in parking lots. That's what the Snowball Dining Room looks like today. Still, I don't know of too many places almost a football field underground, where you can get a hot plate lunch.

Unlike the Historic Cave Tour, where visitors walk to the cave entrance, folks on the Half Day tour are bussed to a manmade cave entrance. Before leaving the VC parking lot, guides gave introductory talks, reminding everyone of the tour's rigors. One guide, a bowlegged Kentuckian named Lloyd Wells, elicited snickers whenever he climbed onto the bus on seventy-something knees to address sitting Half-Day-ers. Younger men on the bus figured if the old codger could walk four miles in the cave, then by God they certainly could. They had no idea that Lloyd could walk the pants off men half his age. I knew this firsthand.

Boom-Boom and I had a full tour—four busloads. We split up the buses, and I bounded up the steps of the first one, turned, and faced off.

In a chipper voice I belted out my best "Good morning." My salutation was met with utter silence.

Some older men sitting up front kept staring at my waist. I regrouped and tried again. "Good morning!" I belted out a second time. Again, my greeting went over like day old Coors. *God, please don't let this be an August tour.*

Although an "August" tour could happen anytime of the year, typically, they occurred in August—the peak month of the summer vacation season. By then, families are worn thin; having crammed in twenty five national parks in two weeks. Characterized by zombie stares, inconsolable infants, arguments about the best camcorder settings, and absolutely no humor, August tours were a real challenge for guides. Too many, and even teetotaler guides would end up taking a nip or two or seven.

The elderly men up front kept looking at my waist and coughing politely, their eyes cast downwards. *Are they trying to tell me something?* Finally, I looked down at my freshly creased National Park Service pants. My fly was open! And it wasn't opened just a smidge. No sir. It was hangar-wide, clearance sale, "Oh look at the Ranger's plaid boxers" open. I turned and hopped off the bus, pulled up the brass, and stepped back on.

"Good morning!" I bellowed for the third time. Cheers rose up. The seniors smiled. I nodded appreciatively.

As the buses rolled out of the parking lot, I struck up a conversation with a couple from Wisconsin. They had a young son named Henry, who was a fifth grader. He wore Coke-bottle glasses and a red University of Wisconsin sweater, with a big, white **W** on the front. His mom said he was interested in bats, especially the much-hyped vampire bat. Of all the bats in all the caves in all the world, vampire bats—the only mammals to feed solely on blood—aroused the most angst. I explained to Henry that vampire bats lived in Argentina, Uruguay and central Chile. He gave me a "yeah, sure" look, and pulled his sweater around his neck in case some hungry, directionally challenged vampire bats showed up unannounced.

The buses rolled over Mammoth Cave's famed Karst topography—a landscape pockmarked with golf ball dimples from the dissolution of limestone—and lurched to a stop in an oval parking lot. Everyone filed off the buses. Chet and I corralled them like sheepdogs into a small assembly area above the cave entrance. Then Chet got up on the rock—guide jargon for leading the tour—except that he was actually standing on a rock. He was the lead guide and I the trailer. It was my job to turn off the lights as we went and make damn sure no one got left behind in the longest cave in the world. Chet began his spiel by first signaling out the smokers in the group.

"Now, folks," he began, "I know Kentucky is a burley state, but I'm gonna ask that you go ahead and light up a half day's worth of cigarettes now, because there's absolutely no smoking in the cave."

Smokers frantically groped for cigarettes. There was a chorus of clicking lighters and striking matches, followed by feverish puffing. People sucked in outrageous nicotine loads, trying to beat the clock. Meanwhile, the "chewers" on the tour—the ones with Skoal cans tucked snugly into their back pockets—smirked. Then Chet followed with his second edict: "Chewing tobacco is permitted in the cave," he said, "but under no circumstances are you allowed to spit."

Chet wrapped up his introduction and stepped down off the rock. Smokers took their last drags, dippers spat out mucousy plugs, mothers herded their children, and dads knob-dicked with camcorders.

One of two rusty, iron doors to the cave entrance had an opening large enough to stick a fist through. I reached in and fiddled with a cold padlock dangling from a thick chain on the other side. The cave air was moist on my skin. Tiny things skittered over my hand.

Admittedly, in my adult life, there've been a few times that I've let out a man-scream. Once was when that guy's head popped out of the hull in *Jaws*. The other was when a Camel Back Cave Cricket danced on the back of my hand as I unlocked the doors on my first Half Day tour. I was with a seasoned Kentuckian when it happened.

He grinned. "Thems crickets."

Cave crickets are one of approximately 130 species of animals that use Mammoth Cave for part of their life cycle. They don't chirp or bite. Despite their large hindquarters, which give them a hunchbacked or "camel-backed" appearance, they're quite docile, though they do leap fearlessly from cave walls onto perceived threats, including humans. I eventually got used to brushing off cave crickets when they tiptoed on my hands and arms, or when they leapt onto the brim of my Smokey the Bear hat like it was a helipad.

Snakes, though, were a different matter, especially during the summer months. Copperheads—a common poisonous snake in the park—favored crevices and overhangs of cave entrances, where they'd bask in the cool fifty-five degree air coming out of the cave. Pencil thick Ring-necked snakes, a harmless variety, also enjoyed the cave's coolness, sometimes dropping from the cave ceiling onto unsuspecting visitors.

I finished unlocking the massive iron doors, and held them open like a bellhop, letting 200 people enter a labyrinth of limestone passages formed 325 millions years ago. The world was different back then. What was to eventually be Mammoth Cave was yet a massive swampland in a vapory climate, later to be inhumed and fossilized into gigantic coral beds. After everyone passed, I locked the doors behind me, and hurried to catch up with the tour. When I did, they were standing in a dry, oval-shaped passageway, etched with scallop patterns on the walls and ceilings—a testament to the sculpting power of water.

#

Trailing guides deviated from protocol with alarming regularity, and often did some "extracurricular exploring" on their own. This was not condoned or encouraged, and there could be serious consequences if the Chief Ranger caught wind of it, but still, it was done. In the brotherhood of cave guides, the axiom, "What goes on in the cave stays in the cave," was fully embraced. It was the NPS equivalent of the infamous Las Vegas mantra.

Once, while trailing a Historic Cave Tour, I tripped over a plate-sized rock. It shifted slightly, and underneath, I discovered a size five sandal woven from plant fibers. The moccasin likely belonged to an intrepid Adena Indian explorer—a pre-Columbian society that roamed Kentucky a hundred centuries before the birth of Christ. It may have even been older than the mummified remains of Egypt's famed King Tut. The beam of my maglite highlighted its exquisite craftsmanship—rows of fibrous strands stitched together to form a sole. Very carefully, I placed the rock back over it. It would be my secret ancient Nike cache. Every time I trailed the Historic Tour, I'd peek under that rock to see if it was still there. It hadn't budged.

Sometimes while "wandering off," I'd come across bundles of smudged cane reed, a bamboo-like plant that grows abundantly along the banks of the Green River—a tributary meandering through Kentucky's cave country. The Adena collected and dried bundles of cane, and fashioned them into torches. The burnt twigs in my hand looked like spent Marlboro's, and begged the question: what happened when their torches went ixnay? Modern day spelunkers use carbide lights, halogen lamps, or battery-powered accoutrements to pierce the dark. The Adena ventured miles into Mammoth's bowels with only fire to light the way. If it went out, well, it went out. *That takes brass!*

Caves can be profoundly muted places. Sitting in the dark, alone, sometimes I'd hear whooshing sounds—blood surging past my eardrums. Veteran guides had told me about this phenomenon, but I didn't believe them. After several minutes of silence, a single thought took on an unexpected tone: "Think you can make it out of here without a light, Dutton?" My voice shattered the deadness like a baseball through a plate window.

My fingers groped for the switch on my Maglite. D-cell light pitifully speared the blackness. I whipped around, half expecting to see an Adena Indian with his hand out… *Give me back my sandal, Ranger.*

#

When I caught up with Chet, he stood around the Diamond Grotto—an exquisite, diamond-shaped gypsum formation, extruding from the cave wall. It was a popular stop on the Half Day tour. Chet stood on a rock adjacent to it. People cloistered around him like he was a quarterback. He talked passionately about the War of 1812, and how slaves toiled in Mammoth Cave, extracting tons of nitrates from cave dirt to make gunpowder for the war effort. I don't think it mattered to him that it had no relevance whatsoever to what they were actually seeing. He finished his gunpowder speech on a patriotic high note— reminding everyone that they owed their American allegiance to microscopic bacteria found in the very cave soil they were standing on.

Henry wiggled to the front of the tour. "Ranger," he began in a high-pitched fifth grade voice, "are the scalloped formations on the walls and roof of this passage caused by limestone dissolution or by wave action?"

Everyone strained to get a glimpse of the whiz kid in the oversized Wisconsin sweater. Chet's strong suit was history, not geology. He stalled long enough until the beam of my maglite hit his chest—the "all-clear" signal that lets the lead guide know everyone is accounted for.

"I think Ranger Dave can better answer your question, young man," Chet said, stepping down from the rock.

I threaded my way to the front of the tour. Henry repeated his question. As luck would have it, just the week before, while on an "after hours" excursion with the park's geologist and some other guides, I asked the same question, though not with the same academic gravitas as Henry.

"Well, like most limestone caves," the geologist said, "Mammoth was formed when subterranean water dissolved the porous rock and then receded to lower levels, leaving behind dry passages with scallop patterns on the rocks, as you see here. It took a lot of time, but limestone is soft, and the water was relentless."

Armed with this knowledge, I dialed up the archival department and punched replay. After explaining the machinations of limestone dissolution, I stepped down off the rock, pleased with myself as Martha Stewart making a Christmas wreath out of backyard pine cones. *Serendipity...it's a good thing.*

Twenty minutes later, the tour entered the Snowball Dining Room. It smelled of steaming chili and corn chips. Henry and I sat down at a picnic table with his mom. He talked geology—bandying about terms like solubility, carbonate and percolation. Not exactly the normal lexicon of a fifth grader. His father approached with a tray loaded with steaming bowls of chili. I excused myself, and went in search of Chet. I found him munching on a P&J. Tiny globs of jelly clung to his red mustache.

"What's with that kid in the red sweater?" he asked.

"You mean Henry?"

"Whatever his name is."

"Well, the kid certainly knows his geology," I said.

"No shit! He makes me feel like I'm on Jeopardy or something." Chet tipped his cup of sweet tea way back.

"We'd hardly got off the buses, and he asks me if I knew the relative age of the cave," Chet said.

"What'd you tell him?"

"Mississippian Period. The kid's a frickin' walking encyclopedia!"

"Don't worry Chet," I assured him, "Henry wants to hang with me. He won't be up front asking you anymore game show questions."

Chet finished the last of his sandwich, gulped down some more sweet tea, and slapped me on the back.

"Thanks buddy. I owe you one."

After lunch, Chet gathered up the tour. Sounding vaguely like the announcer on *The Price is Right*, he peppered his talk with awe-inspiring descriptions of things yet to see—Mt. McKinley, the Grand Canyon of Mammoth Cave, Mammoth Gypsum Wall, Rock of Gibraltar, Onyx Chamber, Frozen Niagara. Henry fidgeted excitedly.

Chet summoned his followers to all rise, and asked that the chili-eaters in the group to please step to the rear. Then, off we went. As Henry and I walked along in a passage that was only an arm-width wide, I pointed out Devonian Era coral in the smooth limestone strata—proof positive that an ancient sea once covered Kentucky. Guides referred to the fossils as "horned corals." The park geologist referred to them as "horny corals."

Henry positioned his coke-bottle glasses inches from the fossil, then declared, "They look like Bugle Corn chips." *Damned if they don't.* Then Henry unexpectedly stopped, and pointed down the passage. Two quivering creatures clung to a limestone crevice, twenty feet from where we stood. Bats! We stood very still, our breathing shallow. The bats were quite small, possibly Eastern pipistrelles, one of the smallest species in North America. Bats usually prefer the solace of remote passages, far from the lights and hubbub of the tourist routes. It was rare to see them this close. After several minutes, the tiny mammals took flight. Slow and erratic at first, they expanded their hands into full wings, and with stretched membrane skin, flitted silently aloft. Henry watched as the bats flew low overhead. Another minute passed. Finally, Henry looked up at me, knowing he'd just witnessed a very private and wonderful thing.

"Cool," was how it came out.

The Half Day tour progressed quicker than a Half Day should. Chet was setting a blistering pace. Things bottlenecked briefly at the base of Mt. McKinley, where a massive collapse of cave ceiling eons ago caused a formidable pile of rock buildup. It seemed strange identifying a high point in an underground cave, where, by nature, everything is already low. Henry and I ascended up nearly 700 feet of rubble. At the summit, drinking fountains and flush restrooms awaited us. The bathrooms were still fully occupied. *This isn't good.* Pods of uneasy cave-goers with anguished expressions waited for a free stall. Henry's mom emerged from the ladies side.

"I guess the guide wasn't kidding about having the chili for lunch," she said to me.

"Mom, we saw some really cool bats," Henry told his mom. "They flew right over us." He put a small hand above his head and made a horizontal slashing movement.

His mother feigned interest, but was clearly preoccupied. Even in the cave light, she looked pale. Henry's mom rallied to catch up with her husband, who was descending into the Grand Canyon of Mammoth Cave. In this section of the cave, the trail is so steep; guides quipped that if you start to slip, be courteous and let out a yell, so that those below can step out of the way as you roll-on by. Henry and I flipped off the bathroom lights and bounded down the trail.

Ten minutes later, we arrived at Grand Central Station—a large chamber formed by the convergence of five tunnel-shaped passages. It was the last stop of the Half Day tour. Quietly, like late arriving parishioners, we took seats on cold wooden benches in the back pew, right behind Henry's parents. From Grand Central Station, it was a half mile to the buses and a ride back to the VC. In between, visitors would see a dizzying array of stalactites and stalagmites, including a massive flowstone formation resembling Niagara Falls frozen in time. The *purtiest* part of the cave, as the Kentuckians called it.

The Grand Central stop was used by guides to wax poetic about Floyd Collins, a young Kentucky caver, who in 1925 became trapped and died in Sand Cave (a cave adjacent to Mammoth). According to legend, Floyd was attempting to find a backdoor entrance to Mammoth Cave, when a rock fell from the tight passage he was in, pinning his foot. For days, rescuers dug to free him, but failed. Their heroics captured the hearts and minds of a nation, and inspired "The Ballad of Floyd Collins," a Grand Ole Opry favorite. When President Reagan visited Mammoth Cave in 1984—the only national park he visited during his two terms in office—he recalled as a boy how he remembered the Floyd Collins tragedy.

After a dramatic telling of Floyd's demise, Chet dimmed the house lights, walked over to an 8-track recorder, and hit the play button. A grainy, Appalachian-pitched voice resonated through speakers mounted atop large rocks in the front of the chamber.

> *...Oh come all you young people*
> *And listen while I tell*
> *The fate of Floyd Collins*
> *A lad we all knew well...*

Henry's mom leaned over and whispered into her husband's ear.

"I have to use a bathroom," she said. I sensed her angst. Her husband though, tapped his feet to the twangy lyric, as if he were listening to an Herb Alpert ditty. Another solemn verse, forecasting gloom and misery, spilled out of the speakers

> *...Oh mother don't you worry*
> *Dear father don't be sad*
> *I'll tell you all my troubles*
> *In an awful dream I had...*

Henry's mom stated her need again to her husband, this time grabbing his shirt.

"What exactly do you want me to do?" he said, in a voice loud enough to qualify as "unacceptable" in a public library. Henry's mom was in the longest cave in the world, miles from any bathroom. "Can you hold it?" her husband pleaded. The ballad grew increasingly ominous.

> *...I dreamed I was a prisoner*
> *My life I could not save*
> *I cried, "Oh must I perish*
> *Within this silent cave...*

Claire stood with balled fists. She was shaking.

"I HAVE TO FUCKING GO NOW!"

Sound carries well in a cave, and people in the front pews swiveled around to see what all the fuss was about.

"Shhh," they scolded sanctimoniously, putting index fingers to their lips, then turning around and pretending they were at the opera. They hadn't a clue the private hell Claire was going through. Claire scowled back at them. Henry's dad turned around and looked at me. At this point, things were unraveling faster than a Sears rug. His eyes pleaded for me to do something, anything. *Yeah, Dutton, you're the Ranger. Do something!*

I stood and asked them to both follow me. "Henry, you stay put," I ordered. I led a bent-over Claire and her husband along the side of the chamber into an adjoining passageway. Henry's mom clutched her stomach. The Ballad of Floyd Collins sounded less folksy and more dirge-like. I yanked a plastic liner from a garbage can and handed it to Henry's dad. He stared back, uncomprehending. Like the Grim Reaper with a Maglite, I pointed in the direction of his wife's cries. He turned and bounded down the passage, plastic bag in hand.

The ballad ended and Chet turned the lights back on. I don't think he was aware that Claire, her husband, and me, were all ahead of him. He slowly led the tour out of Grand Central Station, and past the side passage which concealed Henry's parents. I glanced over my shoulder. They hadn't gone far enough! Henry's mom, still visible, was squatting, her pants bungled around her ankles. Her husband crouched alongside her like a big league catcher, dutifully holding the plastic trashcan liner.

"Hold the fucking bag open!" she shrieked.

Realizing that her backside was now something of a carnival sideshow, Claire began hopping further down the passage. Her husband bounced alongside her, holding open the plastic bag like a trick-or-treater at Halloween. *Oh Jesus!* The bag swung side-to-side like a clear udder. I looked away.

People walked by, craning their necks, watching as the drama unfolded in the side passage. I ushered them along like a traffic cop at a wreck. Not long after the tour had passed, Henry's dad emerged carrying a bulgy plastic sack of dark, swishing liquid, neatly knotted at the top. He handed it to me, which I draped over my arm, like a maître d', concealing it with my Eisenhower dress jacket.

Henry's mom staggered out of the gloom next. She adjusted her horn-rimmed glasses and grabbed her husband's arm for support. Somehow, she managed a smile.

"I'm so sorr—"

"No need to be sorry, Ranger Dutton," Claire interrupted, "you were just doing your job."

Henry, who I'd completely forgotten about, suddenly materialized out of cave air.

"Where have you been young man?" his father asked.

"Checking out a side passage, dad," Henry replied. "I didn't see any bats though." He looked at his mom.

"Are you okay Mom?"

"I'm okay." She hugged her son, and the four of us walked our way to sunlight.

#

It was a punishingly hot day for the guide's picnic—a raucous affair held in late summer, just before the seasonal guides went back to their other lives. The Chief used the occasion to recognize guides for outstanding achievements during the summer. It was a gluttonous affair—BBQ chicken, creamy coleslaw, baked beans, butternut squash casseroles, derby pie, gallons of sweet tea. I was asked to help with the cooking duties, an honor usually reserved for only the Kentucky guides.

I spent a hot afternoon stoking hardwood fires, frying chicken livers in cast-iron skillets, and charring chickens. Cooking poultry over a hardwood fire is thirsty business. Several times an hour, everyone retreated behind a dilapidated shed and poured sour mash whiskey into Dixie cups. We made toasts. To what, I don't remember, and as the afternoon wore on, it mattered less and less. Then it was back to tongs and chickens. We followed this routine faithfully, until our shadows grew long and the festivities were scheduled to begin. By then, we were gassed.

The Chief of Interpretation—a large man who reportedly hated going into the cave—mounted the dais to kick off the festivities. Draped in an immense Hawaiian shirt and wooden beads around his thick neck, he cracked jokes, made speeches and handed out awards. Throughout the evening, guides traipsed up on stage and accepted their accolades. We cooks sat in the back, eating fried chicken livers, and enjoying our hard-earned buzz. At some point, I heard Mary B calling my name.

"Ranger, you'd better get up there," she said. "The Chief's giving you an award."

I slalomed my way around picnic tables, and managed to mount the dais, feeling like Morgan Freeman in a fitted tuxedo accepting an Oscar. The Chief presented me the Scoop Drennan award for my heroics on the Half Day tour. I shook his huge hand and smiled for the paparazzi, sporting a sour mash-induced grin. The Kentuckians hooted and hollered. I took the piece of paper from the Chief, teetered off the stage, and disappeared into the humid night.

At some point, I'm not sure when, Mary B caught up with me. She took my hand and led me home like a lost child. I awoke the next morning face down on the bed, fully clothed except for my shoes, and reeking of wood smoke. Chicken liver grease coated my mouth like Crisco.

"Good morning, Ranger," Mary B said, handing me two jiggers of apple juice. To the hung over brain, there is absolutely no difference between amber-colored apple juice and sour mash whiskey.

I choked down bile, and rushed past her to the bathroom. I heaved, and heaved again, and probably a third time. I collapsed by the toilet, thinking pickled thoughts—a smelly plastic bag, Henry's mother with her pants down, Henry's dad playing catcher. *Poor woman. At least I don't have 200 hundred souls watching me wretch.*

I puked again, then crawled on all fours, like a beaten dog, back to the bed. There was a crinkled piece of paper on the nightstand. I recognized it as the Scoop Drennan Award the Chief had given me the night before.

"Mary," I called out, "do you think we could get a picture frame the next time we're in Bowling Green? I got something to put in it."

I could hear rummaging around in the kitchen.

She hollered back, "Sure Scoop, no problem."

Leaves Don't Lie

"I Feel a Change Comin' On"
~ Bob Dylan

It was a crisp October morning. Man and dog walked along a blacktop road that bordered park housing. Daniel swiveled his pointy ears, listening to a deciduous forest slowly undress. Leaves murmured, no doubt discussing the upcoming leaf pageant on open, windy wavelengths. *Should I wear carotene this year to the leaf ball? Oh no, dear, orange is sooo last year. I'd wear flavone. Yellow looks exquisite on you!*

Halfway around the park housing loop, we paused. A stiff breeze put folds in my plaid shirt. Daniel eased his venerable frame onto his rear haunches, brushing leaves with his swishing tail. His tired, brown eyes spotted a bushy-tailed squirrel ping-ponging in the understory, but the will to give chase had waned. I reached down and patted Daniel's head. *It's okay boy, I know.* The wind in the crowns of wrinkled hickories and bent oaks blew rumors our way. *Changes in your life are coming, Ranger.*

Daniel and I resumed our journey, eventually reaching our one story house with peeling paint. In the front yard, a naked elm drooped over a weathered, stone walkway which led to a rusty screened porch. A spire pipe poked out of a pitched roof, venting aromatic wood smoke into a cloudless, autumn sky. Daniel and I walked up the porch steps and went inside. He went to his water

121

bowl. I went to the bathroom. Mary B sat teepee style on the white tile floor, holding a small plastic wand. She looked up at me as I came in. Light pouring through a battered, four-paned window glistened in her eyes.

"I'm pregnant," she whispered, "you're going to be a Dad."

A huge grin creased my face. I knelt on the floor next to Mary B. She placed a soft hand over mine. We hugged. Daniel entered the bathroom, tail wagging, water dripping from his ashen muzzle. He looked at his mistress sitting on the floor. Inside the tiny bathroom, we formed a joyous, eight-legged huddle. Outside, the leafy telegraph was abuzz...*Gonna be a dad. Stop.*

#

The next morning, I strutted into the guide lounge, a cock-of-the-walk smile stenciled between my ears. One of the guides noticed the rooster in the room.

"What's up, Dutton?" she asked.

"Mary B's pregnant."

"Really?"

"Yeah. And I've accepted a GS-9 Park Ranger job with the Corps of Engineers in Mississippi."

Yesiree. A change is comin'!

90 Days in a Holiday Inn

*I pretend I'm one of the royal family when I'm in a hotel
and that the hotel belongs to me—it is a palace.*
~ Martin Short

Within the federal government, there are five agencies
that primarily manage America's vast public lands—the
National Park Service, the US Fish and Wildlife Service, the
Bureau of Land Management, the US Forest Service, and the US
Army Corps of Engineers. The first three are housed within the
Department of Interior; the USFS is part of the Department of
Agriculture, and the US Army Corps of Engineers is part of the
Department of Defense.

In November 1986, I reported to my new duty station—
the Sardis Lake Field Office, Sardis Mississippi—newer than
a greenstick fracture in the ways of the US Army Corps of
Engineers. I'd left an agency steeped in interpretive traditions, and
joined up with another whose roots date back to the Continental
Army. I had serious regrets about leaving the National Park
Service. I loved the agency. Still do. But, with Mary B growing
bigger everyday, I'd soon have a family to support, and the sad
reality was that I just couldn't support a family on a GS-5 salary
(In 1986, it was $14,800/year). If I stayed with the NPS, I might
rise to the GS-9 level within fifteen years. And that's if everything
worked out. The Corps offered me a GS-9 Park Ranger position,
which I could obtain within two years.

So, in the late fall of 1986, we left Mammoth Cave and the National Park Service, bound for Sardis Lake, Mississippi, 330 miles to the south. We were gypsies in transition; Mary B, a bit rounder; Daniel, a little grayer; Cinnamon, a pinch wiser (about toad snuffling); and me, somewhat drier behind the ears. Our temporary billet was the Holiday Inn in Oxford, Mississippi. For the next three months—while we house-hunted and dealt with the frustrations and nuances of acquiring a VA home loan—two-and-a-half humans and two dogs shared a ground floor room, managing to not step on toe or paw.

Our room was in the rear of the property, tucked under a stairwell, away from the street. It was usually quiet, except when an occasional church bus rolled in, crammed to the rafters with hormone-amped teenagers. Invariably, they occupied the floor above us, slamming doors, and racing the length of the balcony. At night, partying went on, seemingly unabated. Mary B slept through it all. Daniel, Cinnamon and I, however, growled at the nonstop thumping overhead. *Even God rested one day.*

After a particularly boisterous all-night Bible study and calisthenics session, I rose before sunup the next morning, prepared a small urn of hotel Arabica, poured a cup and sat down next to the room phone. Daniel stared at me through droopy eyelids. I dialed the room number directly above us.

After five rings, a voice finally answered. "Hello?" *She sounds like a sleeping angel.*

"This is your five AM wake up call, Ma'am," I said, in my best front desk voice.

"I didn't leave a wake up call," the seraph protested.

"Strange," I said, slamming down the receiver.

I dialed the next room number, and woke up someone else, then the next, and the next, each time sounding more professional. Ten minutes later, the entire second floor rang out in the predawn darkness. My work was done.

#

No cooking was allowed in our small room, so we ate our meals out. At a buffet one evening, everything under the sneeze guard was a lovely mahogany hue, including the broccoli. We sat our trays of food down, and I popped a golden, crisp hush puppy into my mouth. I looked over at Mary B, gnawing on a deep fried frog leg. I think she mistook it for a juicy chicken thigh.

Pregnancy Axiom #1: Never tell a pregnant woman that she is having Kermit the Frog for dinner.

Pregnancy can do weird things to people. Although Mary B was doing all the incubating, I was growing right along with her. Later, I found out the twenty pounds I'd gained during her pregnancy was attributed to an affliction known as Couvade Syndrome, sometimes called sympathetic pregnancy. Luckily, my leather belt had some elasticity to it. But barely.

Throughout her pregnancy, Mary B was obsessed with Mexican food, which became problematic. In the 1980s, the only thing rarer than decent Mexican cuisine in Oxford was an atheist. Luckily, there was a Taco bell in town, and we quickly exhausted the menu, consuming enough gorditas, tacos, beef, chicken, and cheese burritos to fill a cattle truck.

One chilly January evening in 1987, we returned from dinner to find a church bus from Decatur, Alabama, idling in the parking lot just outside our room. Kids with bulgy backpacks ascended the stairwell to the second floor like Sherpas. I could hear Daniel and Cinnamon barking. *Another damned sleepless night?*

We entered our room. Daniel and Cinnamon greeted us with unreserved, tail-wagging joy, and the expectation that we'd bring home leftover tacos. Mary B headed for the bathroom. I lassoed the posse and headed back out into an icy Mississippi night for one last tinkle trot. Daniel and Cinnamon charioted along a street lined with antebellum homes, stately oaks and quaint yards with ornate, wrought iron fences. *Someday, we'll have a house of our own—with a yard and trees.* Crosby, Stills, Nash and Young's warm melody floated into my cold brain "… Our house is a very, very, very fine house…" I deviated slightly from the lyric and substituted two dogs, instead of two cats, in the stanza. The boys finished hosing another pillared gate.

"C'mon guys, let's get out of here."

We hurried back to the hotel. Mary B was already asleep. A light on the room phone blinked. I sat down on the other bed, shaking off the cold. The disciples upstairs had moved on to the sprinting events, doing the ten yard dash with what sounded like concrete shoes. I dialed the front desk to see what the message was.

"This is Mr. Dutton in room 119."

"Oh yes, Mr. Dutton," a young man said. "Someone from Bill King's Realty called while you were out. They said to tell you that the VA approved your home loan."

"Thank you."

I hung up the phone, and burped beef tacos. I looked over at Mary B and Daniel, spooning. I undressed, climbed under the covers, and nudged Cinnamon to the other side of the bed. He growled in protest. Above, as Psalms reached a crescendo, I closed my eyes, and slept.

The Lord truly does work in mysterious ways.

Merthiolate, Tomaters and Slugs

*"To understand the world, you must first
understand a place like Mississippi."*
~ William Faulkner

Working for the Corps of Engineers meant adjusting to a
new agency paradigm. I'd become fully immersed in
a myriad of activities associated with a Corps run park—dam
operations, fish and wildlife management, contracts, public
relations, recreation management, law enforcement, plus a few
more. I was mindful of being a Californian in a land of moon
pies, cotton bolls, Ole Miss and fried okra. Culturally, I felt I
needed a passport, and maybe shots for dengue fever. Yet moving
to Mississippi proved to be one of the best career moves I ever
made. During my tenure as a Park Ranger at the Sardis Lake Field
Office, I embraced adaptability. Sardis Lake had its quirks and
foibles, all parks do, but at Sardis, braggadocio was all but absent
from the day-to-day operations. Rangers and Maintenance
alike possessed a hard work ethos. If you wanted to fit in, you
only needed to roll up your sleeves and "get you some," as my
Southern colleagues put it.

In a cardboard box in our Holiday Inn room, I found a
few wrinkled NPS long sleeve uniform shirts, and finagled
some Corps of Engineers patches to sewn on. Although Corps
of Engineers and National Park Service Rangers have different
agency insignias, they both wear identical gray and olive-drab

uniforms. The Corps accessorizes in midnight-black, whereas the NPS spruces up in cordovan brown. Mary B reluctantly agreed to be my Betsy Ross.

"Make sure you sew the patches on the right shoulder," I said, meaning, of course, the *correct* shoulder; agency insignia always go on the left shoulder.

On a warm afternoon, one week before Thanksgiving, I stood with Frank Walker—the Resource Manager for Sardis Lake—outside the red brick Sardis Lake Field Office. We looked out at Sardis' Lower Lake, two hundred yards away.

"Dave," it came out *Day-ve*, "who sewed your patch?" he asked, pointing to my Corps insignia. I looked at my left shoulder. No Corps patch. *Crap, I meant my other right.*

Just then, a squadron of mature Bald Eagles—their white heads shinning in the late fall sun—took flight over the Lower Lake. I'd worked in Kentucky, New Mexico and California, and up until that balmy afternoon at Sardis Lake, I only needed one hand to count the Bald Eagles I'd seen in the wild. As I watched the eagles arcing low over the water, scattering coots below like billiard balls on a good break, it brought back memories of another large bird I saw once—a California condor.

#

On a lazy Sunday afternoon in October 1980—the kind of afternoon that might include beer and the beach—I sat on a dusty road, overlooking a deep canyon. The occasion was an ornithology field trip. The instructor—a steely-eyed birder who knew every line of *Alice's Restaurant*—trained his Bushnell's on the smoggy brown horizon to the east.

A pickup truck bounced along a rutted road below, dragging plumes of dust with it. The truck reached the canyon's edge where the class had gathered. A young man wearing a straw cowboy hat and denim shirt got out. He explained that his heifers were giving birth in the pasture below and that these red-headed birds with huge wings—he stretched his arms wide, exposing sweat-stained armpits—just started showing up. He asked the instructor if he knew what kind of birds they were.

The rancher's story piqued our attention. Could these large birds be the elusive California condor, one of the rarest birds on the planet? Condors were once abundant in the remote valleys and canyons of California's coast range. They're carrion eaters, and a ripe placenta would be too irresistible for them to pass up. We put down our beers (beer and biologists go hand in hand, like cops and donuts), and scrambled for spotting scopes. Suddenly, an extremely large bird looped into full view. California condors have the largest wingspan of any bird in North America. Even without binoculars, we knew what we were seeing.

More condors levitated up, circling, catching updrafts on wings longer than a one-story building is high. The afternoon suddenly got livelier. Excited expletives rang out. "Fuck, look over there!" "Holy shit, there's another one!" We all watched as three…eight…ten…eventually fourteen California condors with red featherless heads graced the skyline. We could not know it then, but on that autumn day, we may have been eyeing half the known population of California condors in the world.

In the coming weeks, the class took up a collection (basically our beer money) to have T-shirts printed commemorating the sighting. Silk screened across the front of the shirts was a black, white and red California condor, along with the number 14. Below the silhouette of the great bird were the words:

Zoo 323
Oct. 5, 1980

I still have my T-shirt, though strangely, it only fits a teenager.

Long before our record sighting on that October afternoon, the California condor's existence was in peril. Habitat loss and people shooting the shit out of them accelerated their demise. Extinction loomed. In 1987, the remaining wild condors were rounded up and placed into a captive breeding facility, where they ate, slept, watched avian porn, and made condor babies. They got good at it too. The condor population rebounded enough so that biologists could begin tentative releases back into the wild. Today, there are hundreds of California condors, both in the wild and in captivity, and their range is continually expanding.

#

And so, as my boss and I stood with our hands above our brows like Indian scouts in a western, a lone eagle broke formation, and plunged downward. As it lifted out of the water, the sun glistened off a scaly fish clenched in its dark talons. I turned to Mr. Walker.

"Did you just see that?"

"Yeah," he said, as if Bald Eagles were common as beer in a bass boat. He turned to go back into the field office.

"Maybe the project could host an eagle watch this winter?" I said.

Mr. Walker, a tall man, turned around and studied me. Doubt was etched in his face. His large hands nervously jingled change in his pockets. The boss always had pocket change.

"We could invite the public to come out and help us count Bald Eagles," I continued. "Maybe use the patrol boat and count eagles in the upper lake too." I felt like a teenager asking to borrow the family car.

"Day-ve, have you thought this through?"

Well, no, but...

"We don't even have a conference room for folks to gather," he said, sounding like a dad cautioning his son about peckerwood drivers. "What happens if it rains or snows?"

I pictured the two of us standing there—the young, headstrong Park Ranger, and the wise worldly veteran—both with cartoonish balloons pillowed above their heads. Mine read: *What a great idea!* The puffy cloud over Mr. Walker's read: *Is this kid nuts?*

The eagles peeled off and flew to distant trees. Mr. Walker looked down at his young protégé with the Corps patch on the wrong shoulder.

"Okay Day-ve," he smiled, "get me a plan."

Plan?

#

By the time the spring of 1987 rolled around, I'd been at Sardis Lake for half a year. The Vicksburg District was embarking on an ambitious undertaking—tabulating timber volumes for their respective flood control projects. Sardis Lake alone had 60,000 acres of forested lands, all of which would have to be surveyed, tabulated and catalogued. It would prove to be a daunting task. The job entailed not only a rudimentary knowledge of forestry practices, but also knowing what tree species lurked out there.

And so, on a warm April day, I stood on the downstream embankment of Sardis Dam, next to my immediate boss, Supervisory Park Ranger Billie Lee Rawlins. He was slight of paunch, and walked with a swagger that made me think he'd wrestled gators in his youth. He smoked too much and was a proud Vietnam vet. I was too, although the closest thing to Southeast Asia I ever experienced was the jungle cruise at Disneyland. In conversation, Billie Lee referenced Vietnam often.

"You call this a storm?" he'd spit. "Hell, in Nam it rained more than this before breakfast!"

Now, with his long sleeves neatly rolled halfway up his thick forearms—Billie Lee never rolled them past his elbow—he pointed to a grove of leafless trunks. It was early, and the foliage, in the words of my fellow Rangers, "hadn't showed out yet."

"What's that tree over there?" he asked.

"That's a Blackjack Oak."

"Yep."

With a stubby finger, he pointed to another tree.

"What about that one there?"

"Pignut Hickory," I answered, confidently.

Billie Lee raised an eyebrow. He scanned the forest below, looking for a stumper. The pop quiz wasn't over yet, not by a country mile. He twiddled a toothpick in his mouth, which he did whenever he was thinking.

"Over yonder, what's that mohuncher?" he asked.

"That big one next to the Red Oak?"

"Yep."

I studied the tree for ten New York seconds. The striated, grayish bark looked lopsided, like a drunk had pasted long, thin strands of fiber around the trunk. I shot Billie Lee a sideways glance. A "gotcha" grin lit up his tan face. His toothpick froze.

"That's a Hophornbeam," I guessed.

Billie Lee took a step back. The grin vanished from his face. He looked me up one side and down the other, rolling his toothpick until it collided with an unlit Marlboro, which he lit, and exhaled through his nose.

"Damn, Dutton. For a kid from California, you sure know your species." Species came out as *speee-ceees*. Standing on the dam that morning, I may have earned some grudging respect.

One of the oddities about Billie Lee was that he had a unique proclivity to cock up words, especially when he got pissed.

"You Rangers need to be wearin' your gargles," (*n.* protective eyewear, often worn while performing hazardous jobs). The Rangers took to calling it Leebonics, though none of us had the stones to tell it to his face. After staff meetings, we'd rush to our offices and scribble down new sayings we'd just heard. Eventually, we compiled enough to form an unabridged Leebonics dictionary. At my going away party years later, we presented it to him. Billie Lee beamed. He clearly liked the idea that there was a dictionary devoted to his sayings.

Mr. Rawlins was a forester by trade, and was more comfortable traipsing through the woods than being hemmed in by computers. He despised all things administrative, and scolded his young Rangers for being too preoccupied with office minutiae.

"Y'all ain't spendin' enough time in the field," he'd rant. "Someone might be putting *confetti* (*n.* destruction of surfaces, usually by spray painting one's name or slang) on the dam." He had a point.

Billie Lee spent his free time away from the Field Office farming and ranching. On Monday mornings, he'd show up to work looking like he'd been tumble dried with the orneriest, thorniest briar in all of Panola County. His tan arms, hands and sometimes his face were crisscrossed with scarlet scratches, made pink by the application of Merthiolate he'd liberally applied to them. The Rangers paid homage to their boss, presenting him with the first-ever Merthiolate-splattered Certificate of Recognition. He liked it so much; he placed it on the wall in his office.

During lunch in the breakroom, Billie Lee liked to show off his prized homegrown tomatoes. He called them *toe-may-ters,* and was clearly proud of what he'd created. He perfected a routine whereby he'd skin a tomato with his pocketknife, splay it onto a Saltine, douse it with Tabasco, pop it into his mouth, close his eyes, and smack his lips. So much red juice had pooled on the lunchroom table when he was done, it resembled a CSI crime scene. One day, Billie Lee offered me a pulpy tomato.

"No thanks," I said, "I don't do tomatoes."

He looked at me like I had three ears. Truth be told, I can eat just about any tomato byproduct—juice, pizza sauce, ketchup, salsa, soup—but eating the raw deal? *Buddy, forget it.*

One afternoon in the lunchroom, Billie Lee was going on about some yahoos who'd high-centered their pickup along a muddy backroad near his house. As he told the story, he pulled a massive tomato from his lunch box, and began ritualistically skinning it. Another Ranger pulled up a chair at the lunch table, and emptied the contents of a wrinkled paper bag. Out rolled a tomato the size of a cannonball. Billie Lee's eyes bugged out like a frog.

"Jimmy, where'd you buy that tomater?" he asked.

"Didn't buy it," Jimmy said, smiling, "picked it this morning from my garden."

"The heck you say!"

"Yessir. Grew it myself."

Everyone stared at Jimmy's monstrosity. *Larger than anything Carol Doda ever displayed on stage, that's for sure.* It was, hands down, the largest tomato we'd all seen in the lunchroom. Compared to Jimmy's tomato, Billie Lee's looked like a ball bearing. That day in the lunchroom, Jimmy hadn't just laid down the tomato gauntlet; he'd metaphorically slapped Billie Lee across the face with it. There was a new Tomater King in town, and everyone knew it.

Billie Lee, though, wasn't about to relinquish his hard-earned title as the best gardener in Panola County. No, sir. Not without a fight. The following week, he strutted into the lunchroom with a tomato that resembled a small crimson melon. It must've broken the back of the poor plant that gave birth to it. Billie Lee centered it on the lunch room table like it was the Lombardi Trophy.

Jimmy just smiled. He didn't say a word, although he knew he'd been bested. Somewhere in his viney garden though, lurked a botanical aberration aching to be purloined. The next week, Jimmy brought in a colossal red ball that would've won best of show at the Mississippi State Fair. Any horticulturist would've been proud to mount it over the fireplace in the den, alongside the twenty-point buck. Lee kept his head down. He didn't say a word.

And so it went. Back and forth all summer long, each man trying to best the other. By first frost, the great tomato fight had gone the distance. When all the scorecards were tallied, Billie Lee, by a split decision, retained his title as Tomater King.

And who says males aren't preoccupied with size?

#

In the early winter of 1991, I approached Billie Lee with a request. He was working on the Ranger schedule, and per usual, looked damned annoyed.

I pulled up a chair. "Billie Lee," I began, "as Sardis' Interpretive Ranger, I'd like to attend the National Association for Interpretation workshop this year."

He looked up from what he was doing. "Let me clearify," (*adj.* to make plainer). "You got this on your IDP, Dutton?" (IDP is Governmentese for Individual Development Plan. In the government, everyone supposedly has one, but if they were on a library shelf, they'd be in the fiction section).

"Yes, sir," I answered.

"Where's the training?"

"San Jose, California."

Billie Lee put down his pencil. He eyed me suspiciously, like I was in a police lineup. His toothpick glided across his lower lip, then back again. I didn't say anything.

"All right, then. Get with Louise and set up some travel orders," Billie Lee said, finally.

"Yes, sir."

I was going back to Cali, my home country. Maybe I'd get an infusion of west coast vibe...*California dreamin' on such a winter's day...*

On the Monday morning following the workshop, I drove to work preoccupied with one thing—how to convince Billie Lee to bring the Banana Slug String Band to Mississippi? The musical group had headlined the San Jose workshop, and brought the house down with their unique blend of music, theatrics, and puppetry. Selling the idea of bringing the band—guys with nicknames like "Airy" Larry, "Solar" Steve, Doug "Dirt" and "Marine" Mark—to Mississippi, wouldn't be easy. I walked into Billie Lee's office, pulled up an ass-worn GSA chair, and dove right in.

"Billie Lee, I've got an idea."

He leaned back in his chair, locked his stocky hands behind his neck, and looked at me, hard.

"Well, it figures. You go out to California and come back with some harebrained idea." Idea came out *idear*.

Undeterred, I continued. "I think we should try to bring the Banana Slug String Band to Ole Miss. Possibly combine the event with some environmental education workshops for teachers. We could bus kids—"

Billie Lee put up his leathery hands. "Whoa! Stop right there. Banana who? You want to string what?"

His chair came forward, and he put his elbows on his desk. His long sleeves were partially rolled up his thick forearms, revealing numerous Merthiolate-doused scratches. *Must've been a bad rose weekend, huh?*

I took a deep breath, and regrouped. I explained all about a group of talented musicians and environmental educators I'd seen at the NAI Conference. They called themselves the Banana Slug String Band. I didn't mention their stage names. I talked about a noticeable gap in environmental education in Northern Mississippi, and how bringing the Slugs to the state could help with that. Finally, I explained how we could partner with Ole Miss as a venue to make it all happen.

"It would be great PR for the Corps," I added.

Billie Lee's hard stare softened. "That ain't very pacific, Dutton (*adj.* to be very detailed in an explanation)."

"I'm still workin' on it, but I think it's a good idea." I said *idear,* to get him on my side.

"Well, okay then. Get me a plan, and I'll take it up with Mr. Walker."

"Thanks, Billie Lee."

I walked a short distance up the hallway to my office, picked up the phone, and dialed Santa Cruz, California. After two rings someone picked up.

"Hello," a Banana Slug answered.

Fourth of Joo-Lie

"There's only two reasons for a Ranger not workin' the
Fourth of Joo-Lie: yoor dead or yoor gettin' married."
~ Billie Lee Rawlins, Supervisory Park
Ranger, Sardis Lake Field Office

It's a given that Park Rangers work the Fourth of July holiday.
It's the busiest recreational holiday of the year, and possibly the
deadliest. While Americans celebrated the country's founding
with elaborate picnics and double-dyed fireworks, I celebrated
by dealing with drunks, boating accidents, lost children,
overcrowded campgrounds, runaway campfires, or, sadly,
drowning. In the summer of 1987, I sat in a hot, cramped field
office, listening to our crusty Chief Ranger, Billie Lee, chastise his
inexperienced Ranger cadre.

"There's only two reasons for a Ranger not workin' the
Fourth of Joo-Lie," he sneered, "yoor dead or yoor gettin'
married."

That afternoon, I drove home thinking…*My wife is due any
day now.*

Three days later, on July 1st, Mary B rolled over in bed and
touched me on the arm.

"My water broke," she whispered in the dark.

I stiffened upright. In a nanosecond, I went from REM
sleep to triple espresso awake. While Mary B gathered her things,
I dressed, and poured some kibble for Daniel and Cinnamon.
They stood in the kitchen with "Waz up?" expressions. Then,

Mary B and I set-off for the Oxford Lafayette Medical Center on the far side of town. I drove cautiously, never exceeding the posted speed limit by more then 30 mph.

At the hospital, they whisked Mary B into the inner sanctum. Three hours passed. I poured cup after cup of hospital coffee into ridiculously small Styrofoam cups. I paced and peed for another hour. Finally, the doctors determined the baby would be delivered by caesarean section. A nurse handed me some blue scrubs. I put them on, feeling like Dr. Kildare.

The doctor that would perform the C-section walked into the room, yawned, ran a hand through a mop of disheveled black hair, and poured a cup of coffee.

"Whew," he recoiled, "coffee is strong this morning." I shot him a look. *Better be, Doc. Have another cup. That's my wife in there!*

He shuffled off, leaving me to my pacing. I'd worn a track in the linoleum floor by the time a nurse ushered me into the OR. Mary B lay on the operating table draped in blue napkins. She had on a face mask with tubes sticking out of it that made her look like an Air Force fighter pilot. In the time it took to change a flat, the doctor made an incision, briefly rummaged around in Mary B's belly, and pulled out a baby girl. At 9:52 AM, on July 1, 1987, Katherine came into the world. She had a top knot of black hair, and a Beaujolais-colored birthmark shaped like a butterfly on her right hip. No amount of scrubbing by the nurses made it come off. They took her over to her mother, then wrapped her in a towel and handed her to me. I counted all her toes. She looked at me. My heart vaporized.

The news that our baby daughter was jaundiced—a yellow discoloration of the skin caused by a buildup of a substance called bilirubin in her blood—shocked us both. "It's called hyperbilirubinemia," the doctor explained. "It's common in newborns." *I knew I shouldn't have smoked that weed in college.* "It's treatable using phototherapy," the doctor continued, "she's going to have to stay in the hospital another couple, three days, though."

Two days passed. The next day was the Fourth...*Only two reasons for a Ranger not workin' the Fourth of Joo-Lie...*I watched, palms pressed against the nursery glass, as Kate lay naked under blue lights, wearing only black velvet eye patches. *She looks so alone.*

I turned and walked down the hall to the nurse's station, and asked to use their phone. I had to speak with my boss. Billie Lee picked up on the second ring.

"Billie Lee, I'm gonna need the fourth off."

There was a pregnant pause.

"My daughter is jaundiced. She needs to stay in the hospital a few more days."

"She's john-what?"

"She's jaundiced," I repeated, louder. "She's kind of yellow."

"Well, that ain't good."

"The doctor says her bilirubin count is high, and they're trying to get it down to safe levels."

"Billy-who is high?"

"Bilirubin," I repeated.

Another long pause. "Well, you take care of that youngin', hear? We'll see you when you get back."

"Yessir."

I handed the phone back to the nurse, and walked down the hall to Mary's room. For the first time in my Park Ranger career, I wasn't going to suit up for the fourth. I could almost hear Billie Lee's raspy drawl as he addressed the Rangers at the next staff meeting.

"There's only three reasons for a Ranger not workin' the Fourth of Joo-Lie: yoor dead, yoor gettin' married, or yoor havin' a kid."

The Lady No One Could Say No To

I imagine that yes is the only living thing.
~ e.e. cummings

"**A**re there any questions?" I asked the group of volunteers huddled around me like a football coach. Our billows swirled in the icy, predawn air, like bison in a Yellowstone winter. Two dozen volunteers gathered in a parking lot across from the Sardis Lake Field Office for Sardis' first annual Bald Eagle Watch. Sporting puffy coats and thick-fingered gloves, they sipped hot coffee poured from Army National Guard field canteens, and shuffled their feet to stave off cold. In the back of my mind, I could hear Mr. Walker's wise words…*We don't even have a conference room for folks to gather in…*As I distributed the forms to record Bald Eagle sightings on, a woman in the back of the group piped up with a question.

"Mr. Dutton," she began, "how do we know we're not counting the same eagles twice?" Her voice was slightly sweet, vaguely assertive, and undeniably Southern.

Beanied heads swiveled my way. I pulled my fur trooper tighter over my frozen ears. *Damn good question.*

#

At just a scootch or three above five feet in height, with sparkling brown eyes and combed, dove-gray hair, Mrs. Dorothy

Bartlett Wingo, the lady who asked the question, was sixty-five years old when I first made her acquaintance that frigid morning in 1987. I was thirty-one. A rookie Corps Park Ranger doing my best to conduct the project's first Bald Eagle watch. Over the next twelve years, Mrs. Wingo—I always called her Ms. Wingo— would take me under her wing, and watch as I fledged.

Politically, Ms. Wingo and I were color opposites—she of the cardinal persuasion, me of the bluebird variety—yet somehow, we managed to avoid dipping into the politico, even when the entire country was frothing about Mr. Clinton getting his wick dipped in the White House. Nature, though, seemed to be the glue that bonded us, especially if it came with a beak and feathers. Whenever I was in Sardis doing Corps business, I'd swing by Ms. Wingo's duplex on Hightower Street. We'd watch birds of all stripes flit to her bird feeders which hung like *piñatas* from the many trees in her backyard. Whenever a rascally corn snake showed up uninvited, she'd hurriedly place a call out to the field office.

"It needs catchin', Mr. Dutton."

"What needs catching, Ms. Wingo?"

"The snake! It's eatin' my birds!" Ms. Wingo didn't believe in killing snakes.

"I'll head over just as soon as I can, Ms. Wingo."

Ms. Wingo's interest in Sardis Lake predated my arrival there by almost half a century. Shortly after Sardis Lake became operational in 1940, she, her husband Bryson, and some close friends, would fish it often. After Bryson's death in 1970, Ms. Wingo sought solace in the convivial pleasures of birding, and quickly became adept at it—ably discerning the subtleties between an immature male Merlin and a Peregrine Falcon from 100 yards.

My own interest in birding took longer to develop. When I was twelve or thirteen, one of the neighbor kids, BG, and I, went on an afternoon safari with his shiny new BB gun he'd gotten for his birthday. I lined up its stubby sight, and slowly squeezed off a round. One hundred feet away, a bird fell like a plumb bob from its perch on a pine branch. We stared in disbelief, then ran over to the tree. On the ground lay a limp English sparrow. I'd shot it right through the eye; a one-in-a-million shot. Holding it up by its tiny toe, I didn't really feel like a crack shot. I felt shitty.

BG's dad, Mr. Nelson, got wind of our hunting expedition and decided that the killing presented a teachable moment. We were to cook and eat the sparrow, presumably as punishment. We plucked feathers and scooped avian intestines in my mom's kitchen. I was fascinated with the crude necropsy. I'm not sure this was the outcome Mr. Nelson envisioned.

We ended up with two Lima bean-sized breast patties that we braised in butter, and ate along with some corn chips. After that, we never shot at neighborhood wildlife again. Instead, we tested our marksmanship on Colt 45 cans, lemon trees and plastic toy soldiers—only the German and Japanese soldiers, though.

#

Following the Bald Eagle Watch in 1987, Ms. Wingo became increasingly involved in the project's upstart volunteer program. The volunteer hierarchy at the Sardis Lake Field Office from 1987-1998 resembled something like this:

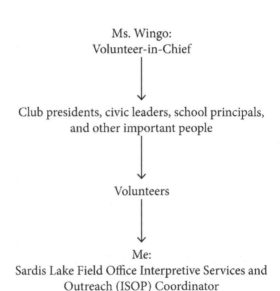

Ms. Wingo:
Volunteer-in-Chief

↓

Club presidents, civic leaders, school principals,
and other important people

↓

Volunteers

↓

Me:
Sardis Lake Field Office Interpretive Services and
Outreach (ISOP) Coordinator

If a modal synapse occurred anywhere between the hierarchal tiers, then Sardis' volunteer program—one which eventually accounted for 7,500 man-hours annually—would've gone south. But it never did, in large measure due to Ms. Wingo's tireless efforts. Whenever the Corps held community-sponsored events at the lake, first call I'd make was to Ms. Wingo. She'd seek people out with the zeal of a recruiting sergeant. Folks in Panola County had two choices whenever Ms. Wingo called: arrange a funeral to attend, or just say "yes."

A few years after Sardis' inaugural Bald Eagle Watch, the Sardis Lake Field Office underwent a facelift. The remodel included new offices and a spacious conference room. Now, instead of gathering in freezing darkness, eagle watchers mingled under soft incandescent lights and warmed their dorsal sides against wall-mounted heaters, while sipping decaf tea. Participants started showing up for the event armed with sugary confections and colorful vegetable trays. The Eagle Watch was becoming *avant garde*. During the tenth annual Eagle Watch—a survey that resulted in a record thirty-four eagles being spotted—T-shirts were made to commemorate the event. A three-tiered cake topped with a Bald Eagle was commissioned for the occasion. Ms. Wingo brought a delicious Chess Cake she'd made, and watched with a maternal glint in her eye as I piled yet another piece onto my paper plate.

#

One September afternoon in 1993, just after our Lakeshore Cleanup Day, I heard Mr. Walker coming down the hallway. I could tell it was him because he had a habit of rattling his large knuckles on the walls as he walked along. I was in my office writing thank you letters to the 400 volunteers who showed up for the event. The rapping stopped at my door. I looked up. Mr. Walker's tall frame owned the threshold.

"Day-ve," he announced, reaching into the jelly bean bowl on my desk, "I'd like to put Mrs. Wingo in for an award."

I put down my pen.

"Yes, sir, I agree. What award do you suggest?"

He paused, although the jelly bean intake continued, unabated.

"Well, I don't know, but a good one. I'll leave the write-up to you. We'll need to get 'er done before the end of the FY." *Shit boss, the fiscal year ends…next week?*

He turned and left my office, leaving behind a barren candy dish. The knuckling moved one door down to the Engineering Tech's office. The boss wouldn't find any candy there though; the Engineering Tech was a prodigious tobacco chewer. The only thing on his desk, other than technical manuals and fine print reports, was a red plastic Solo cup, stuffed with paper towels and mucousy, week-old plugs.

After Mr. Walker's dictum, I walked up the hall to the clerk's office, and asked Louise if she had information on the Army awards program. She took a long pull from her Diet Mountain Dew, reached for a dusty pamphlet on the shelf above her computer, and handed it to me. I carried it back to my office, closed the door, and plunged into the wonderful world of Army Regulation 672-20: Decorations, Awards and Honors, Incentive Awards.

An hour later, I discovered what I thought would be a worthy award for Ms. Wingo—the Commander's Award for Civilian Service—the third highest civilian honor in the Department of Defense. According to the Army manual, Chapter 8, Honorary Awards, section 8-5, sub paragraph *c*, sub-heading *(1) …eligibility for the award is based upon level of achievement, including accomplished supervisory or nonsupervisory duties in an outstanding manner, setting an example of achievement for others to follow…*

I tried to absorb that. For over two decades, Ms. Wingo had served as the Panola Playhouse production coordinator, was the President of the Rose Hill Cemetery Trustees in Sardis, and had designed the gardens for Sardis' nursing home. *Was that not setting an example of achievement for others to follow?* For the Annual Lakeshore Cleanup Day, Ms. Wingo recruited volunteers from throughout the Mid-South—from the Mississippi Delta to Memphis, Tennessee.

Still, it would be a heavy lift. The Department of Defense (DoD) didn't hand these awards out like candy. As I compiled documentation for the write-up, I wasn't concerned so much about disappointing my boss (though incurring his wrath was not a pleasant thought), as I was disappointing Ms. Wingo. She deserved recognition. She'd earned it. It was up to me to make sure she got it. As the fiscal year clock ticked down, I hunched over my desk like Bob Cratchit over his ledgers, scribbling and re-scribbling, composing and recomposing.

One challenge in writing the Commander's Award wasn't in quantifying Ms. Wingo's achievements—in 1993 alone, she'd logged over 500 volunteer hours at the Lake—the challenge would be in *qualifying* them. Ms. Wingo had championed citizen involvement and environmental stewardship for six years. It was not a stretch to say that Ms. Wingo was the bedrock of volunteerism at Sardis Lake.

On Monday morning, I presented the award nomination to Mr. Walker. He read it, looked up, and smiled.

"Day-ve, you did good." Praise like that coming from Mr. Walker was as good as it got.

"Thank you. Do you think it will fly in Division?"

"Oh yeah."

The award nomination did, in fact, sail through the review processes of the upper echelons of the Corps, and on a short-sleeved afternoon in mid-October, Mr. Walker and I stood on a grassy knoll overlooking the Lower Lake. A smiling Ms. Wingo stood sandwiched between us dressed in a spiffy exercise outfit. The top of her silver, coiffured hair barely reached the creased breast pocket of Mr. Walker's shirt. She and Mr. Walker held a corner of the gold-framed Commander's Award for Public Service. They smiled for the camera, as Cris Fletcher, the editor of Sardis' hometown newspaper, rolled film. The front page headline in the October 21, 1993 issue of The *Southern Reporter*, read:

Dot Wingo honored
For volunteer work

#

Post Script: In June of 2010, around the same time the Lakers and the Celtics were squaring off in the NBA Finals, and twelve years after leaving Sardis Lake, I attended a Corps interpretive workshop in Huntsville, Alabama. By then, I'd worked my way up the ranks and was an Operations Project Manager at Abiquiu Lake in Northern New Mexico. I was as Mr. Walker was; only now, Park Rangers came to me asking for the car keys. After the class ended (and the Lakers walked away with their 16th NBA title), I rented a car and drove west through the verdant Alabama countryside. I crossed the Mississippi state line at Fulton, and two hours later pulled into the parking lot across from the Sardis Lake Field Office. It hadn't changed one iota.

Twenty-three years earlier, I'd stood in this same lot huddling with a group of frozen eagle watchers, including Ms. Wingo. The Bald Eagle Watch was still going strong. Who knew counting Bald Eagles would have so much staying power? After jawing with some of the Ranger's I used to work with, trying to cram twelve years of memories into a few hours, I got back into the rental and headed west toward the town of Sardis.

Twenty minutes later, I pulled into the driveway of a quaint duplex on Hightower Street. The smells of fresh cut grass, honeysuckle, and jonquils in bloom, blended with songbird choruses, concocting a potent nexus of smell and sound. Ms. Wingo pushed open her screened door, and invited me in. Her eyes were still as vibrant, her hair as perfectly configured, as when I first met her. We sat in her modest living room in overstuffed chairs, drinking lemonade and reminiscing about our days at Sardis Lake. We laughed a lot. We always did. Everything in her house was neat and orderly, and fit like a jigsaw puzzle. Mounted conspicuously on the wall in her living room, was her framed Commander's Award.

We walked out onto her porch, glasses of lemonade in hand. It was a warm afternoon, and Ms. Wingo's yard resembled an avian tarmac. Brightly-feathered warblers caroused in treetops, while spectacled vireos with distinct eye-rings poked among low shrubs, plucking spiders with stubby bills. Pugnacious wrens with loud timbres also hopped about, terrorizing insects. We stood quietly, taking it all in. Then Ms. Wingo turned to me, and said something I'll never forget.

"Mr. Dutton," she began, "all those years I volunteered out at the lake were some of the happiest times of my life."

There was just the tiniest glint of a tear in her eye. I didn't know what to say. We stood on her porch awhile longer until it was time for me to go. I turned and gave Ms. Wingo a big hug, then hopped into the rental car, waved goodbye, and sped north up I-55 to the Memphis Airport to catch a plane bound for Albuquerque.

Two hours later I was 30,000 feet over Arkansas, eating salty peanuts and looking out the window at pureed water vapor. I suppose some might find it odd that a man would have an ongoing friendship with a woman thirty-four years his senior. Outside of their own mothers, none of my friends have such a friendship. There is no doubt that my life has been enriched for having befriended Ms. Wingo. I've often wondered how my life, how my career really, would have been different, if she hadn't asked me *that* question on a frigid morning in 1987?

And that, Ranger, is a...*damn good question!*

The Darkest Cloud

Tut, Tut! It looks like rain
~ Winnie the Pooh

Ranger Hunter and I stood in Mr. Walker's spacious office, enjoying the cool air conditioning. Our uniform shirts were plastered to our backs. It was an August Mississippi day—hazy, hot, and humid—the dreaded 3 H's. Mr. Walker sat at his GSA desk, surrounded by voluminous Operations and Maintenance three-ring binders and dusty engineering blueprints held together with aging rubber bands. His back was to a large picture window that looked out on Sardis' Lower Lake. The walls of his office were studded with framed pictures, certificates and awards, all slightly askew. Mr. Walker talked to us about the project's water safety program. I'm not sure I was listening too closely. I was more focused on the evil storm that was congealing behind his back.

As Mr. Walker talked, strobe flashes pulsed within a mucosal cloud, like a static electricity lamp at a science fair. Furious downdrafts suddenly churned the Lower Lake into a giant foamed latte. Families on the beaches packed up coolers and umbrellas, and scurried for the safety of their cars. Bank fishermen reeled in their casts. Boaters exposed in open water, raced for shore as fast as their outboards would propel them, hoping the jagged spears of light would not pierce them. Thunderclaps boomed with artillery-like intensity, rattling everything, especially Mr. Walker's picture window. He swiveled in his chair in time to see rain gushing from the dark cloud like a broken water main. "Good God!" he exclaimed.

Ranger Hunter's radio crackled to life. "Man down! Man down!" It was the project's electrician, and he sounded scared. Ranger Hunter keyed the mike on his lapel.

"Charlie, what's your 20?"

"Paradise Point Beach. Two guys down. Might be dead, I don't know. I need fucking help!"

Radio protocols didn't allow for cursing on park channels. Whatever Charlie saw couldn't be good. Ranger Hunter and I bolted from Mr. Walker's office, sprinting down the linoleum hallway to our own. I grabbed my radio and keys to the van. What I failed to grab however, was my CPR pocket face mask, or even a rain slicker. We jettisoned out of the motor pool, heading west along State Highway 315 enroute to Paradise Point, about a mile down the road. Water surged across the two lane highway. The van's windshield wipers were all but useless. *Might as well be driving in a goddamn waterfall!*

I barely saw the exit for Paradise Point Beach, or Charlie standing in the deluge with his Corps hard hat, yellow slicker, and shin-high rubber boots, pointing in the direction of the beach. Through the downpour, I could just make out two bodies lying facedown on the sandy beach. Both bodies were close to a park bench that was under a thickly crowned Loblolly Pine tree.

Later, I found out lighting scored a direct hit to the tree's crown, injecting millions of volts of electricity down its cambium and through its roots, which unfortunately, were in contact with the metal pipe footings of the park bench. Electricity coursed through the men's bodies, launching them both twenty feet.

I rushed over to one man; Ranger Hunter ran to the other. I knelt in a puddle, and rolled him over. He was young, maybe in his early 20s. His eyes looked dead. I checked for breathing using a head-tilt, chin-lift technique to open the airway. He wasn't breathing. There was no pulse. I opened the man's mouth to begin CPR. In an instant, the pelting rain filled it like a coffee cup.

I was a trained EMT, Basic Life Support, and CPR instructor, but nothing prepared me for this. I splashed out the rain, and breathed into his mouth. Air gurgled in, and the pushback inflated my cheeks. His chest rose. I shifted to his torso, locked my wrists and elbows, and compressed his chest up and down in piston-like fashion. The cascading rain was so loud, I couldn't hear myself counting compressions. I shouted...

ONE-and-TWO-and-THREE-and-FOUR-and-FIVE-and-SIX-and...THIRTEEN-and-FOURTEEN-and-FIFTEEN

You're working on a dead man, Dutton.

Other Rangers materialized out of the torrent like watery ghosts, and took over chest compressions. No one, it seemed, wanted the head. Somebody, maybe Mr. Walker, stretched a poncho over us, which made it much easier to administer rescue breaths. At least the man's mouth wasn't a wading pool each time I parted his lips.

I hunched over to give more breaths. A sickening upsurge of hot, alcoholic vomit filled my mouth. *Fuck!* I recoiled, turned my head, and heaved. I sat there for a few moments in the beating rain, catching my breath. Charlie later told me that before the storm hit, he'd seen the two men enjoying a six pack. I turned the man's head to the side, and scooped sticky phlegm from his mouth with my fingers. He was most likely dead, but if he aspirated vomit into his lungs, he surely would be.

I can't recall how long I performed CPR. Fifteen minutes? Twenty? I was exhausted and saturated to the molecular level, but I couldn't stop. Finally, two Sardis EMS units arrived, the incessant rain all but muting their blaring sirens and pulsing red lights. Everyone helped load the men into the ambulances. I climbed in with my man. The technician quickly inserted an airway, then handed me a CPR face mask with an air port and an Ambu bag. I strapped the face mask to the patient, attached the Ambu bag to the valve, and squeezed it hard, forcing air into his lungs.

It was soupy hot inside the cramped confines of the ambulance. Evidently, the air conditioning wasn't working. As we struggled to keep the man alive, stinging sweat dripped into my eyes. We continued CPR, rolling with the rhythms of the ambulance, until suddenly, the ambulance sputtered and jerked, slamming us both to the floor. *Are we stopped?* The technician banged angrily on the wall of the cab with his fist.

"Go, go, go, Goddamnit!"

I looked down at my man. His eyes were as vacant as stones. The driver cranked the ignition for the umpteenth time, but as with the patient, the battery was also dying. Then, a spark arced across a plug, and the engine fired. It coughed, swallowed, coughed again, and grudgingly choked down gas. The ambulance lurched onto the highway, throwing us to the floor for the second time. And then, it broke down—again. The town of Sardis is approximately nine miles from Sardis Dam, about a ten minute ambulance ride. We were on the long end of thirty minutes, and counting.

When we finally arrived at the hospital, the EMT and I rolled the stretcher into the ER. I was still compressing. My arms were numb. A doctor emerged, placed a stethoscope on the man's naked chest, and listened.

"Stop CPR," he commanded.

For a moment, no one said anything. Except for the beeping of a monitor on the wall, the ER was silent.

"He's gone," the doctor said, solemnly.

He instructed the nurse to record the time of death. He thanked us for our efforts, and left the room. I turned and shuffled into the tiny ER waiting room, head down. When I looked up, a short woman with frizzy hair stood in front of me. Her eyes were deep, searching pools.

"She's the mamma of them two boys got killed at the lake," the ER nurse piped up. "She's a deaf mute."

I looked at her. *How do you tell a deaf mute her boys are dead?* The woman searched my face, watching my mouth.

"I'm sorry," I said, loudly. "Your sons are gone." I couldn't bring myself to use the word dead. *She can't hear what you are saying, remember Dutton?*

Her face contorted horribly. Tears raged down her cheeks. In her grief, she made gut wrenching, animal-like sounds. I stood there for a minute, wet and exhausted, totally ill-equipped to comfort her.

"I'm so sorry," I said again, and headed for the exit. I had nothing left to give.

The air outside the hospital was thick and muggy. The storm had passed, and the sun was high. It shone on the leftover wetness, turning it to steam. I stood in the parking lot, reeking of vomit and sweat, an emotional skeleton, stripped bare by fear and grief. What I wanted was to shed my stinking uniform, take a long, cool shower, and rinse my mouth with a tall whiskey. *Is this the dark side of being a Park Ranger?* I turned away, covered my face, and wept.

#

About a month after that horrible August afternoon, the Corps held a ceremony at the Sardis Lake Field Office to recognize the Park Rangers that helped in the ill-fated rescue of the two men. Mr. Walker presented me with an ivory-colored certificate with a gold, embossed eagle centered on it. He started reading the citation: *"David A. Dutton is officially commended for the performance of his duties as Park Ranger in the Sardis Lake Field Office on 17 August 1989. Mr. Dutton went far beyond the normal call of duty in attempting to save the life of an individual who had been struck by lightning at Sardis Lake..."*

I saw Mr. Walker's lips move, but didn't hear his words. In my mind, I was squatting in monsoonal rain, puking, counting "one-and-two-and-three-and-four-and..." I was in a hot ambulance staring into a lifeless face. I was in a sterile, waiting room, desperately wanting to avoid a mother's mournful wails. I was in all of these places—again.

Mr. Walker finished reading the citation. I shook his sizeable hand, and reclaimed my seat. I didn't feel pride. I didn't feel accomplishment. I felt empty. Somewhere out there was a grieving mother with two less children.

#

Postscript: In 2002, thirteen years after the killer storm at Sardis Lake, the Corps initiated the Critical Incident Stress Management Program. Known as CISM, it recognized that Park Rangers perform dangerous missions, and that "Many of these missions require that employees be exposed to incidents, accidents, fatalities and large-scale disasters."

Any Park Ranger that has ever worked a drowning (especially a child), or a drowning recovery (especially where the victim gassed off and bobbed to the surface weeks or months later), or a boating accident (especially involving propellers), or a fatal car wreck, or a shooting, or any traumatizing event during his or her career can pretty much recount everything about it. God help the Park Rangers that have seen so much death, they no longer can.

'Em Are Ducks

Be like a duck. Calm on the surface, but always
paddling like the dickens underneath.
~ Michael Caine

It was an unusually warm March day in 1987—one that begged for short sleeves, and fly swatters. The mosquitoes were waking up, and they were hungry. Billie Lee stormed into my office. He'd just smoked a cigarette. I could tell, because whenever he did, his veins fanned out across his cheeks like red fishermen's nets.

"Goddamn sap's risin', Dutton," he spat.

"What?" It was one of many colloquialisms I'd come to know during my twelve years at Sardis Lake.

"Some yahoos buggered up Clear Creek last night. Spray painted everything in sight. Happens every time the sap rises in the spring. Night Ranger's said beer bottles was everywhere." Billie Lee was clearly pissed.

"Sons of bitches probably drank themselves into bolivia (*n.* drunken state). I'd sure like to catch 'em just once. Just one goddamned time! I need you to go on up there and check it out. Take some pictures. Got me?"

"Yessir."

I finished up a report for Mr. Walker, then climbed into my van and headed for Clear Creek, a remote recreation area in northwest Lafayette County, about an hour drive from the Field Office. I drove with the windows down, enjoying the balmy air.

Red wasps flew in and lounged on the vinyl dashboard before jettisoning out the passenger window like Hollywood stunt doubles. Vandals are elusive fuckers, scurrying around under the cloak of darkness carrying spray cans, and "buggering" things up, as my boss put it. Few things piss off Park Rangers more than wanton destruction. Replacing vandalized property siphoned scarce Operations and Maintenance dollars from an already meager budget.

Fifteen minutes outside of Oxford, the road dipped low into Toby Tubby Creek bottom, a place where Cypress trees grew in thick, stout clusters. Suddenly, a flash of color streaked low across the road in front of me. I recognized it as a male Wood duck—a bird with such riotous coloring, it rivaled stage dancers in a Las Vegas show.

Wood ducks (*Aix sponsa*) are considered the most colorful of North America's waterfowl. Male Wood ducks have candy-apple red irises, which compliment their iridescent green, blue, purple, white, bronze, black and chestnut-colored feathers. They possess sharp claws, toenails actually, that allow them to perch on tree branches. Few ducks can pull off such a high wire act. Extensive market hunting of Wood ducks in the late nineteenth century caused their numbers to dwindle precipitously. Their brilliant feathers were prized by fly fishermen for trout flies, and were also a smash hit with the ladies' hat market in Europe. Extensive logging coupled with the draining of wetlands in the early twentieth century, also led to considerable loss of their habitat.

In 1918, Canada and the U.S. decided it might be a good idea to keep these birds around, so the Migratory Bird Treaty Act was hatched. Hunting Wood ducks became illegal. With the advent of artificial nesting boxes in the 1930s, and better agricultural practices (less draining of wetlands), Wood duck populations rebounded, and hunting them became legal again, though you couldn't take as many home for dinner.

#

I continued driving another twenty minutes and eventually reached the Clear Creek Recreation Area. The place had been tagged extensively. I took pictures, got back in the van, and headed back to the field office. When I reached the bridges spanning Toby Tubby Creek—the place where I first saw the male Wood duck—I pulled over, got out and peered over the bridge. Biochemical goings-on in the inky, placid waters below could not mask the musky pungencies above it…*Ol black water, keep on rollin'*…A Diamondback water snake pushed and pulled its bulky body along a slippery bank. Swirling swamp gnats rushed ahead of the serpent, hoping for a rotting fish to lay their egg payloads. Dark water sluiced around bulgy-bottomed Cypress trees, and wherever logs protruded out of the water, turtles (locals called them cooters) climbed on, looking like stacked dinner plates in a cupboard. In the muggy air of the bottoms, I heard the sounds of swamp amoré—baritone Bullfrogs jug-a-rumming, male songbirds shrilling, and the *oooo-eeek* of a female Wood duck in flight, as she streaked through a tangled understory, calling out for her mate.

I stood on the bridge for ten minutes, absorbing the swampy sights, sounds, and smells, then climbed into the van and headed back towards Oxford. I was running late, but I had an idea I needed to flesh out first.

Fifteen minutes later, I pulled onto the campus of the University of Mississippi. Backpack clad students scurried about campus, walking under Dogwood trees in full bloom. Towering red brick buildings with white ionic columns watched the procession, as did ubiquitous, bushy pink azaleas. I parked in the rear of the Exercise Science and Leisure Management building, and got out thinking exercise was something you either did reluctantly or maybe obsessively. I was somewhere in between.

I found the faculty office of Dr. Charles Chase, and walked in. My plan (*Day-ve, get me a plan*), was to have student volunteers build Wood duck nesting boxes, and place them in prime watersheds around Sardis Lake. Dr. Chase was French-Canadian, stout and rugged, even with a tie. He was a man who knew his way around a wood. He'd grown up in Minnesota, hunting and trapping. As luck would have it, he and a colleague, Dr. Jim Gilbert, were heading up an outdoor education class, REC 569, and were looking for opportunities to funnel students into experiential learning activities. When I told Dr. Chase what I wanted to do, he beamed. My proposal would segue nicely into their program.

Back in the van, I headed west toward the Sardis Lake Field Office. I drove into the motorpool, just before quitting time. Billie Lee's blue pickup with his lariat looped over the backseat gun rack was still parked in the lot across the street. He was working late. I parked the van, went into his office, and pulled up a chair. Billie Lee pushed aside a stack of papers on his cluttered desk, and lit a cigarette—which was *verboten* in the building. I don't think he gave a shit, though. I think he could have started a controlled burn right then and there on his desk. He was having a rough day.

"Well, how was Clear Creek?" he asked.

"It was like the Ranger's said it was…pretty messed up. They tagged a lot of signs, especially down by the boat ramp."

"Sons of bitches," Billie Lee snarled, and exhaled a billow of smoke.

I debated about making my pitch about my plans for an Ole Miss volunteer program, or wait until later. I decided on the former. Billie Lee had graduated Magna Cum Laude from the "School of Hard Knocks," and he would know just how laborious my proposal would be. He listened as I talked about putting Wood duck nesting boxes around the lake, using students as mules.

When I finished my pitch, Billie Lee said, "Well, they're certainly young and vicious." (*adj.* eager; seeking higher status). Might be good for 'em. Get me a plan."

"Yessir."

I called Dr. Chase the next day, and told him we had the green light for the project. Two weeks later, on a drizzly morning, Drs. Chase and Gilbert, some graduate students, and me, all donned chest waders, and entered the wet wilds of Toby Tubby Creek. We would end up doing what the students affectionately called "Duckmucking." We spent hours shooing away curious snakes and determined mosquitoes, and chose two dozen prime locations for Wood duck hotels. Not long after, I followed up with a delivery of Cypress planks to Dr. Gilbert's house on campus.

The design for our Wood duck nesting boxes came from an old Mississippi Department of Wildlife, Fisheries and Parks pamphlet. The boxes were heavy (made with one inch rough-hewn Cypress), and slightly bigger than a mailbox. They had overhanging roofs, circular front holes for nesting access, and side-hinged doors near the top (to count Wood duck eggs). For the next two weeks, students gathered at night in Dr. Gilbert's small garage, sawing, hammering and assembling nesting boxes. By early April, twenty-five Wood duck nesting boxes were complete and ready for placement in the field.

Just before the boxes were finished, I paid another visit to Dr. Gilbert's workshop. This time, I unloaded rolls of twenty-four inch wide aluminum sheeting to wrap around the trees the nesting boxes would be mounted on. The slippery sheeting was meant to discourage nimble raccoons or snakes from climbing up to the nesting boxes and feeding on the eggs inside. That was the theory, anyway.

#

When it comes time to fledge, Wood duck chicks transform themselves into feathered alpinists. At their mother's urging, they use their hooked toes to ascend to the opening of the nest, then hurl themselves to the water below. That's the easy part. Bullfrogs, gluttonous snapping turtles, and wiley water snakes all await them, mouths wide, like trick-o-treaters waiting for Halloween candy to drop. Some Wood ducks never make it out of the embryonic stage, instead becoming avian Slurpees by marauding raccoons or voracious rat snakes. Whoever coined the phrase, "Mother nature is a bitch," probably had Wood ducks in mind.

One year after the volunteer project began, the University of Mississippi, Sardis Lake Cooperative Outdoor Education Project (try saying that three times fast), had cycled through one complete nesting season. Student observations and collected data indicated the Wood ducks were using the nesting boxes at nearly 100 percent occupancy. I kept Billie Lee abreast of developments, and told him about all the students' sweat equity.

"Well, that's good. At least they ain't drinking alkehol (*n.* intoxicating liquid), and buggering up rec areas."

Just before spring break, I called Dr. Chase to see if he wanted to go Duckmucking again. He needed to check on the student's progress, so the two of us ventured into the wilds of Toby Tubby again to do some spring reconnaissance of our own. At the first nesting box, I squared the extension ladder against a stout Cypress tree and climbed up. At the top I peered into a dark nesting box. I never expected to be nose-to-nose with a sleepy raccoon. I'd heard the glorified accounts of students finding coiled, Anaconda-sized rat snakes, or Eastern Screech Owls, or hordes of Red Wasps, or even flying squirrels in nesting boxes. But never was there a mention of a raccoon. I recalled lunchroom conversations with Rangers about how a desperate, treed "coon" could shred a hunting dog like confetti. Now, a raccoon's moist, black snout was just inches from own, and it was twitching. My options were limited: try to close the hinge without getting my face ripped off…or jump.

"What's in the box, Dutton?" Dr. Chase shouted up. He sensed something was amiss.

At that moment, I turned my head and looked down at him, offering an ear for the taking rather than my eyes. The frightened raccoon scurried out the side opening, unleashing a torrent of piss as it raced up the trunk to an overhanging branch. Viscous, stinky urine cascaded down, saturating my shirt. I finished counting the eggs in the nesting box, and climbed down the ladder, smelling like a sotted hobo.

"Phew," Dr. Chase said, reining in the extension ladder, laughing.

We trudged on through the duckweed to the next nesting box. Dr. Chase positioned the ladder against a chunky Tupelo tree, and motioned for me to climb up.

"No, thanks," I declined, "your turn."

#

The heck you say: Three years and 2,000 volunteer hours later, the Ole Miss volunteer program was honored by the Mississippi Take Pride in America (TPA) program, and twice captured national TPA awards in the Educational Institutions category. In July 1990, Drs. Chase and Gilbert, several undergrads, and I, all traveled to Washington, D.C. At the awards after party, Dr. Gilbert posed with his lifelong heartthrob, actress Linda Evans, who happened to be the Take Pride in America Spokeswoman that year. The undergrads, wearing spiffy ties and coats, hobnobbed with the Secretary of the Interior, Manuel Lujan Jr., while Dr. Chase and I shared a brew with sausage magnate Jimmy Dean, also a TPA spokesperson. We were, as my southern brethren might put it, "In tall cotton."

I'd like to say that the Ole Miss Wood Duck study became a national model for Corps of Engineers reservoirs with waterfowl management responsibilities, but that would be a lie. What I can say is that adding much needed housing for Wood ducks at Sardis Lake, also added much needed heft to the résumés of three undergrads who participated in the program. Today, all three are nearing the back nines of their Park Ranger careers with the US Army Corps of Engineers.

And to think...they owe it all to a little 'ol duck with wicked toenails and sporting more colors than a deluxe box of Crayolas.

Black and White

*I have no color prejudices nor caste prejudices nor creed
prejudices. All I care to know is that a man is a human
being, and that is enough for me; he can't be any worse.*
~Mark Twain

A new school year was starting up for the children of Lafayette
County, Mississippi. Harried city drivers stared impatiently
at white-gloved crossing guards shepherding children in
crosswalks, while out in the county; drivers lagged behind
plodding yellow school buses that stopped at every railroad
crossing. Pods of kids shouldering bright backpacks and wearing
their back-to-school best, waited in the predawn for rides to
school.

As I drove across town to pick up my carpooling partner,
I was especially mindful of this. We'd only been carpooling
about a week, and I don't recall his name, only that he'd recently
transferred to Sardis Lake and that when he climbed into my
Nissan Sentra, his bulk punished the seat springs.

We weaved slowly through Oxford's oak-shaded streets
talking shop until we stopped at a popular intersection. A woman
in a bright neon vest walked a group of excited black children
across the street. As the youngsters skipped past, my passenger
grew ever agitated. Finally, he turned to me, and said, "Watch out
for them nigger kids, Dave. They'll run under your tires."

What the? Did he just say what I thought he said?

I turned and glared at his neck folds. He returned the glare.
"You don't think so?"

I stared dead ahead, white-knuckling the steering wheel.

"That's got to be the most ignorant fucking thing I've ever heard anybody say. You and me...we won't be carpooling anymore. Better find yourself another ride home."

He looked like he'd been punched in the face. Even at full-bore, the air conditioning did little to cool my pan-hot ears. The silence between Neck Folds and me grew deafening. I reached over and switched on the radio. NPR correspondent Ofeibea Quist-Arcton was talking about trouble in the Sudan. *Why not just drive his fat ass out in the county somewhere, beat 'em with a tire iron, throw 'em in a ditch and let the kudzu cover him up? Nobody but the Klan would give a rat's ass!*

He folded his arms across his axe-handle wide body and grunted. *Reading my mind, Fatso?* He didn't say another word for the duration of our half-hour commute to the lake. Neither did I.

When we got to work, I went straight to my office that I shared with Ranger Hunter. He looked up when I came in.

"Burl was trying to get you on the radio," he said.

"What did he want?"

"Some yahoo shot at one of our signs again. Burl's working on it, but wanted you to come down to the shop and have a look."

"That's the third sign this month," I said. *Great, a racist prick and a serial sign murderer, all in one morning.*

As the lake's sign coordinator, these things fell under my purview. I climbed into my van, and drove to the maintenance yard—a sprawling compound surrounded by chain link fencing, topped with strands of barbed wire. I got out and entered a large, aluminum-sided warehouse. Burl, a black man with biceps that made The Hulk's look modest, squatted next to a large recreational sign on the shop's concrete floor, pounding out bullet holes. The brown sign came from Coontown Crossing; a remote Corps managed day-use area, very popular with Lafayette County locals. Likely, a pissed-off hunter with a high power rifle perfectly centered two bullets in the side-by-side OOs, making them look like owl's eyes.

Burl was no stranger to hard work. One day, while I dug holes to put up signs for a special event, Burl drove by in his maintenance truck. He watched as I toiled, stabbing at the hard ground again and again with the posthole digger, each thrust yielding a pitiful cup of dirt. Burl got out of his truck, walked over, and yanked the digger from my hands, brushing me aside like a matchstick.

"You might knows about book learnin' Mr. Dutton," he said, "but you don't knows shit about digging no hole."

In ten minutes, Burl finished what would've taken me an hour—three perfectly sculpted, knee-deep holes. He handed me back the posthole digger. I looked at the tiny red blisters on my palms. Burl and I were from different worlds.

"Thanks," I shouted, as he drove off.

As Burl pounded out the bullet holes, Joe, another black maintenance worker, stood over him mumbling advice. Joe was always thinking, always working the angles. In conversation, he always got the last word. Everyone at the lake knew that. Joe pulled a stubby, unlit cigar from his mouth. "I don't know why you bother fixin' that damn sign. Somebody's just gonna fuck it up again."

Burl tried to ignore him. But when Joe said something else, something about the sign being right back in the shop tomorrow, he threw down his paintbrush. He'd had enough. I had too. My day started out pretty shitty, and I wasn't even caffeinated yet. I skirted the edge of the sign ahead of Burl, and stood toe-to-toe with Joe. He pulled the cigar from his mouth and bowed out his considerable chest. We glared at each other like a couple of dogs with their hackles up, getting ready to sniff each other's ass.

"Joe," I said, staring him dead in the eye, "you're the most optimistic motherfucker I've ever known."

Joe's lower lip stood down. He didn't say anything. The only sound in the shop came from a ratty, window-mounted air conditioner. Finally, Burl broke the standoff.

"That's the onliest time I never heard Joe say nothin'," Burl said, laughing.

It was a deep-honed laugh, nothing pretentious. I started laughing too. So did Joe. Soon, all three of us stood around the bullet riddled sign, laughing at the ridiculousness of it all.

"Fuck it, Joe, let's get some coffee."

I drove back to the office just in time for the weekly staff meeting. JT, another black maintenance worker and mechanic at the Sardis Lake Field Office, stood outside the conference room, twirling a Tootsie Pop. His mammoth hand dwarfed the candy in his cheek.

"Good morning, JT," I said.

"Hey Dave, did I ever tell you how I used to pick cotton all day?" For some reason, JT relished telling me stories about his life.

"No, I don't believe so."

JT grinned and started in. "Well, sometimes, we'd be all dusted up when they sprayed DDT from planes. We was all covered in that shit. Almost made me look white," he laughed. For a big guy, it was surprisingly high-pitched.

JT continued. "We got our water from a cistern, but it had all these wiggly worms swimmin' in it." I assumed he was talking about mosquito larvae. "We used coal oil to kill 'em. Had to scoop it aways so's to get a drink. Tasted nasty." JT scrunched his face.

"Damn JT, between DDT and coal oil, your life expectancy is right at eight hours."

#

On a hot September afternoon, about a month after the "Coontown Crossing" incident, I pulled into the maintenance yard. A fish fry was in progress. I smelled it driving in. Catfish, cornbread hushpuppies, mayonnaise-laden coleslaw, creamy Nilla wafer banana pudding and gallons of sweet tea were all up for grabs. I joined some of the Rangers gathered around a bubbling cauldron; jawing and watching hushpuppies bob up and down in hot oil. Football season was starting up. Ole Miss and the SEC dominated the conversation.

I listened awhile, then chimed in. "Cal Poly's looking strong this year. Put a real hurt on Cal State Northridge." The Rangers around the hushpuppy pot stopped talking and looked at me like I had an STD.

"What? We play more than fucking ping-pong and beach volleyball out west, you know."

Their eyes rolled, then it was back to SEC football. Out of the corner of my eye, I spotted Burl and Joe approaching. The circle widened to accommodate them. Burl was smiling. Joe wasn't. Burl spoke first. He looked my way. "What's that you said to Joe the other day, Mr. Dutton?"

SEC football went away. Burl's question piqued the Ranger's attention. I knew what was coming next…"Joe's the most opstimickstics motherfucker you've ever known.'" This elicited a round of laughs, except for Joe.

"Well, shit," Joe spat.

"C'mon Joe," I said. "Let's go get a bowl of Nell's banana pudding."

#

On an oppressively hot August day, when Kate was just over a year old, we headed out in our new Dodge Caravan for Water Valley, Mississippi—home of the annual Watermelon Carnival. The yearly event attracted visitors from around the state. A half-hour later, I parallel parked along a shady side street. As Mary B and I walked over cracked sidewalks, we were serenaded by tone-deaf cicadas. Kate, riding high in her backpack, played with her mamma's hair. The humid air was juiced with slow cooked brisket, fresh cut grass and chemical toilets.

Two blocks later, we reached the fairgrounds. Sticky fingered children ran around with pinky snow cones, while others pecked at towering beehives of cotton candy. Parents shouldered camcorders or pushed baby strollers, while coeds in tight Ole Miss T-shirts wandered about with their clueless boyfriends in tow. Grandpas and grandmas sat on park benches in the shade, fanning themselves with watermelon-shaped, cardboard cutouts. Along the side streets, stake bed Fords loaded to the gills with huge green and white-streaked watermelons, begged to be unloaded. Everyone called them Crimson Sweets, and their flesh was the most sapid I'd ever put in my mouth.

In the center of the grassy park stood an ornate, white gazebo, which served as command central for the carnival. It housed several fold-up tables, chairs and a microphone that the organizers used to make important announcements: **Parents, please do not let your children hang from the Port-a-potty doors!**

After a pit stop (I didn't encounter any hanging kids), I strutted across the lawn next to the grandstand. A short, round man in suspenders crossed in front of me and mounted the gazebo steps. He took off his straw hat, mopped his shiny brow with a red handkerchief, and breathed into the microphone.

"Let us pray," he announced.

Growing up in California, we prayed at church, or around the dinner table. Occasionally, I prayed when I really, really cocked up, like the time I wrecked the family car for the second time in two months. I took off my Sardis Lake ball cap, and bowed my head, offering my neck to the Sun Gods.

"Dear Lord," the man began.

I glanced at the smart people standing in the shade. The short man at the microphone was an equal opportunity blesser. He blessed the watermelons, the growers, the folks in attendance, the Chamber of Commerce, the children, the food, the earth, the sun, and the skies overhead. *Merciful Lord, might there be a way to speed this up just a little? It's freakin' hot out here!* Rivulets of sweat trickled down my back. The all inclusive blessman however, seemed to be just warming up.

"And Lord," he continued, "shower your blessings on this year's Watermelon Court." *Good time to hit the fast forward button Lord, don't you think? Rain would be nice.* The Watermelon Court included Petite Miss, Tiny Miss, Little Miss, Miss Preteen, Junior Miss, Miss Teenage and, finally, the Watermelon Queen herself. *Christ, no wonder Mississippi does so well at Miss America Pageants. Training starts at birth!*

"Amen."

The microphone went silent. The man in suspenders stepped down. Those left standing scuttled for shade. I headed for the snow cone booth. After a blinding brain freeze, I caught up with Mary B and Kate. They were checking out an eclectic crafts booth. Kate bounced excitedly in her backpack when she saw her daddy coming. Her cheeks were rosier than the pink ball of ice I held in my hand. She reached out with tiny hands. I plucked some sweetened ice and fed her small bits like a baby bird. She smacked her lips, and puckered her face. She wanted more. *Wait till you graduate to an It's-It!*

"Ranger, look at all this stuff," Mary B whispered.

In front of us, spread out on various-sized tables, was an emporium of brightly-colored watermelon knickknackery— crocheted pink and white trivets, red embroidered dish towels with black seeds, dishware with red centers and green edges, pottery, wreaths, and pitched-roofed birdhouses, all fashioned to look like colorful watermelon slices.

Two dolls caught my eye. They were stitched in midnight black cloth, with white crisscross diapers pinned in the front. I picked up the girl doll, which fit easily in my palm. Her spiky yarn hair, white painted circles for eyes, and bright red O for a mouth, reminded me of Mr. Bill, the Play-Doh character from Saturday Night Live. Except Mr. Bill was white. I put the doll down next to a collection of hand sewn toaster covers that looked like black mammies straight out of *Gone with the Wind*. Their faces had white buttons for eyes. Red kerchiefs, knotted in the front, covered their heads, and they had the same beet-red lips as the black dolls.

"What kind of Buckwheat, racist shit is this anyway?" I said to Mary B. She looked at the little dolls with bright red lips.

"Have you ever seen stuff like this before? I asked her.

Mary B shook her head. She'd not seen anything quite like it either. She tugged at my sleeve, trying to get me to move away, before I said anything to the proprietor.

"C'mon Ranger, let's get a slice of cold watermelon."

It was late in the afternoon when we drove back to Oxford. We were full of watermelon, cotton candy and pulled pork sandwiches. Kate slept in her car seat. In the front seat, her mother nodded sleepily, swaying with the rhythms of the road. Cool AC blew wisps of her auburn hair. I couldn't get the little black dolls out of my head. I'd never seen anything like that before. It triggered a memory from when I was about ten years old.

My Grandmother—a sweet woman who made two-story high lemon meringue pies—came to visit us one summer. We were all watching an episode of "Gunsmoke" on our black and white TV in the family room. Marshall Dillon was transporting a black prisoner back to Dodge to stand trial. The two men sat around a studio campfire. The black prisoner asked the lawman to take off his cuffs, "So's I can eat," he said. The Marshall weighed his options, then, with trepidation, slowly reached down to uncuff his shackled prisoner. Ominous background music built to a crescendo. Everyone knew the black man would pull a fast one on the unwitting Marshall. At the last possible moment, my Grandmother leaned forward in her chair and blurted, "Don't trust that nigger, Marshall!"

Dad sprang out of his Naugahyde recliner quicker than Jack Lalanne doing jumping jacks. "Mary Ann," he scolded his mom, "you can't say that!"

There were two things about that moment that I distinctly recall. I never knew my Grandmother's name was Mary Ann. And I'd never heard her say anything mean. Later, mom told me that Grandma had grown up in a tough Philadelphia neighborhood, in a generation where everything had a label—coons, spics, paddy's, dagos, crackers. Maybe it was a generational thing. I don't know.

For a middle class white kid growing up in Southern California, television, sadly, was pretty much the extent of my race relations. That changed when the family moved to the eastern fringes of the San Fernando Valley. I was in the seventh grade, and was bussed to a predominantly black junior high school. On the day some asshole shot Dr. King with a hunting rifle, rioting broke out at the school. Fires broke out, and in the melee, my head got smashed into a locker. White kids, some bloodied like myself, got escorted by police to waiting school buses. It was scary.

After high school, I joined the army, and ate, slept, and trained with men of different backgrounds and colors. In Germany, I shared a small barracks with a fiery Puerto Rican named Domingo Zayas. On Friday nights, Domingo's buddies would show up armed to the teeth with Puerto Rican rum and Spanish guitars. We passed around the *bumbo*, strummed and sang like shanghaied sailors, sometimes carrying on till dawn. Except for the commode-hugging which inevitably followed, I enjoyed our all-night debauches.

Then came a spring evening when a black PFC put a knife to my throat outside the Enlisted Men's club. I'll never know if I was the intended target because I was white, or I was just unlucky enough to be coming out of the EM club that night. Maybe he had too much hashish, or whiskey, or both. I was just glad to walk away with my carotids intact. I never held any malice toward the guy.

Then...Mr. Neck Folds, my blobby carpooling partner. He wasn't around the previous summer when I tried to save the life of a twelve year old black girl, who'd been run over by a man driving a truck. Her name was Heather Walton. The girl's family was enjoying a July 4th picnic at Sardis Lake, when Heather chased a ball into the highway adjacent to the picnic area. Witnesses said a pickup truck cart-wheeled her into the air like a rag doll, landing her on her head. I arrived on the scene minutes later. Onlookers crowded around Heather's limp body. The Rangers struggled to keep everyone back. I knelt by Heather's side. She had a pulse, but wasn't breathing. I began rescue breaths, and for forty-five minutes I breathed for her. EMS finally arrived, scooped her off the sizzling asphalt, and whisked her away. Heather was later airlifted to St. Jude Children's Hospital in Memphis, and placed on life support.

About a week after the accident, I decided to drive up to Memphis to check on her. A nurse informed me the family took her off life support the day before. Standing in the sterile hospital room, I thought about Heather lying on the hot asphalt, struggling for her life. I turned and walked out…*Watch out for those nigger kids, Dave. They'll run under your tires.*

As I turned into our driveway on North 9th Street, Mr. Sonny, our next door neighbor, sat in his carport, enjoying a Marlboro. He smiled and waved at us as we pulled in. Mary B went into the house with Kate, and let Daniel and Cinnamon out to do their business. I walked over to Mr. Sonny.

Mr. Sonny was a retired telephone repairman who'd served in Patton's army. He was a good man that would gladly give you the shirt off his back. Occasionally though, during our carport get-togethers, he used racial slurs, which always left me feeling uneasy. Daniel came around the corner of the house and cocked a leg on Mr. Sonny's brick carport.

"Daniel," I scolded.

"No, no, he's fine," Mr. Sonny corrected me. "I don't mind having 'ol Daniel around. Keeps the niggers away."

I was wrestling with Daniel's collar, pretending I didn't hear what he'd just said. But I had. And it bugged me. A lot. I dragged Daniel back to the house, thinking maybe I should have said something this time, not just let it go like I always do. Then a thought occurred to me: am I seriously going to lecture an older white man who'd spent his whole life in the South on matters of race? *Marshall Dillon probably would've, and have done it well, too!*

Then again, Marshall Dillon was a fictional character on a TV show, and had writers to write his lines. I wasn't that fortunate.

Water by the Numbers

Evaporation, condensation, precipitation,
The water cycle boogie goes
round and round.
The water cycle boogie goes
up and down.
~ *"Water Cycle Boogie," Banana Slug String Band*

Throughout the spring of 1991, it rained pitchforks and hammer handles at Sardis Lake. Swollen rain clouds, pumped with Gulf moisture, dumped precipitation over Sardis' 1,545 square mile watershed almost daily, filling up the lake alarmingly fast. When Sardis Lake was constructed in the mid 1930s, the designers calculated that it could hold back 1,512,000 acre feet of water—approximately 482,000,000,000 gallons—give or take a gallon. When that much water backs up behind a dam, it's scary.

A common measurement associated with water management is cubic feet per second, or cfs. Unless you are a mathematician or a Sears appliance salesman, you probably don't think three dimensionally. Try to picture a box one foot wide, one foot tall, and one foot deep—that's one cubic foot. Sardis Dam, in the spring of 1991, let out water at a rate of almost 10,000 cubic foot boxes every second—enough to fill eight and a half Olympic-sized swimming pools in a minute.

In dam safety classes, I would often hear old school engineers say, "When it comes to dam safety, nothing beats a pair of eyes reasonably attached to a brain." Throughout the sloppy spring and into the early summer, men decked out in yellow rain slickers, sloshed up and down the ninety-seven foot high, three mile long dam, looking for signs of seepage—sometimes referred to as piping.

Piping is to a dam what cancer is to living tissue. It manifests through seep water carrying soil particles in solution, and most often appears when there is high water. If uncorrected, it can hollow out conduits. As a rule, holes in a dam are not usually helpful.

As the maintenance crews tended to the dam, Rangers patrolled the impounded waters behind it. During the first trimester of the great flood of 1991, an already pregnant Sardis Reservoir grew even more, inundating all of its 263 miles of shoreline. Floodwaters covered roads, recreation areas, boat ramps, soybean fields, and even a highway bridge or two.

With the high water, came the anglers. I've never really understood the lure of high water, but it seems to attract fishermen like Hare Krishnas to airports. As Sardis Lake filled up, turtles and snakes also sought high ground. It wasn't uncommon to see sliders stacked like china plates, adrift on soggy logs in the floodwaters, far out in the lake. While on patrols, I talked with fishermen who told me tales about epic battles they had with snakes (always monstrous in proportion) that had plopped into their boats from overhanging tree limbs. It always ended badly for the poor snake. *What's so heroic about clobbering a snake with the stout end of an oar?* They were probably just pissed-off their beer got knocked overboard in the melee.

One day, I noticed something peculiar bobbing in the water a few yards offshore. It was a basketball-sized mass of red fire ants (*Solenopsis invicta*). The miniature insects onboard the USS Invicta (Latin word meaning unconquered) scurried over one another, collectively moving the ball closer to shore. It was amazing to watch them. It would take much more than a little flood to stop these tenacious ants. I guess that is to be expected of a species from South America that got shanghaied in ship ballasts enroute to the port of Mobile.

#

Along the northern shore of Sardis Lake, where the Little Tallahatchie River is blunted by Sardis Dam, there is a 400-foot long concrete structure known as the Emergency Spillway. At some point during my tenure at Sardis Lake, the term "Uncontrolled Spillway" replaced "Emergency Spillway," maybe because it sounds less frightening. To my mind though, there are fewer things more controlling than a dam, except maybe the IRS, or a man with his TV remote. Calling the Spillway "Uncontrolled" somehow sounds less reassuring.

But I digress.

The purpose of the Uncontrolled Spillway is simple—to siphon floodwater and prevent overtopping of the main dam itself. In the 1930's, while the storyline for Sardis Dam lay strewn on drawing boards in a cramped engineering office, its designers calculated that water would crest the Uncontrolled Spillway once in a hundred years. Perhaps their crystal ball was cracked. In 1973, thirty-three years after the dam became operational, floodwaters poured over the Uncontrolled Spillway. Ten years after that, in 1983, it happened again, and in early April of 1991, the dam looked poised to spill over a third time.

#

As it turned out, Sardis Lake wasn't the only thing growing in the spring of 1991. Mary B was too. She was pregnant with our second child. As the incessant rains pounded the roof of our house, Mary B readied the nursery and waited. Then, early on the morning of April 30, 1991, perhaps around the same time that floodwaters first lapped over the Uncontrolled Spillway at Sardis Dam, she rolled over in the bed and whispered into my ear, "My water broke."

I dressed, and went into the kitchen. Mary's mom, who'd come out from California to help, was fixing Kate some breakfast.

"You're going to have a baby brother soon," I said, kissing her soft head. She seemed pleased, and went back to her Cheerios. Mary B and I set off for the Baptist Memorial Hospital, North

Mississippi, which was still on the far side of town, only under new ownership. Again, I drove cautiously, never exceeding the posted speed limit by more than 30 mph.

At 7:52 AM, on April 30, 1991, Logan was born. The same doctor that delivered Kate performed the C-section that pulled her little brother into the world. He weighed eight pounds, had blue eyes, and like his older sister, was yellow.

This time however, the hospital sent us home with blue lights to help break down the bilirubin in his tiny bloodstream. He'd have to be watched 24/7, but in two days, he wouldn't look yellow anymore. We drew straws. I got the 2:00-4:00 AM shift. I sat in a rocking chair in the baby's room, looking at my son curled up in a ball. Like his sister, he too wore black protective eye patches. I wanted to pick him up, and hold him. A cold rain pelted the window outside, but inside, the electric coils of a wall-mounted heater glowed orange, making the room toasty. I rocked gently, back and forth in the rocking chair. *What will become of this boy?* Cinnamon lay at my feet, sleeping with one eye open, like a pirate. Since Logan's homecoming, he'd been a four-legged security detail, always vigilant around the baby. A gentle knock on the door rousted me from my stupor. Cinnamon gave a low growl. My mother-in-law peeked in. My watch was up. I shuffled back to bed, hoping to grab a couple of hours of sleep before work. Lying in bed, I heard the rain slamming the house, and then I didn't.

The alarm roared to life at 6:30. I rolled over and slapped it silent. When the snooze went off, I slapped it again, and again, and again. After a hot shower, I dragged on a wrinkled uniform and shuffled into the kitchen. I filled the *Presto* percolator with cold water, shoveled in Folgers, and set the electricity to it. As it gurgled and sputtered, I stared out the kitchen window at another bleak, rainy day. Finally, the amber light on the coffee pot winked. I poured steamy coffee into a travel mug, and poked my head into the baby's room. Mary B and Logan were as one. I smiled, and headed out again into the perpetual wet.

Thirty minutes later, I pulled into the parking lot across from the Sardis Lake Field Office, and got out. I walked down a long corridor to Billie Lee's office, dripping. Sitting in a well-worn chair, I stared bleary-eyed at him from across his wide GSA desk. A drop fell from my ball cap and splashed onto his desk calendar. He stopped what he was doing, shifted his glasses to the tip of his nose, and peered over them at me.

"You look like shit, Dutton," he said.

"The hospital sent us home with a portable light system. My boy is jaundice. He's got to be watched 24/7 till he gets better. I really need a couple days off, Billie Lee."

"Shit Dutton, again?" *Why do I feel like he thinks my kid is retarded?* A toothpick shifted nervously from one side of his mouth to the other. He was mulling over my request.

"Sorry, Dutton, I can't approve any leave right now," he said. I stared back, blankly.

"We got a flood fight goin' on," he continued. "I need every swingin' dick out there patrolin'. Maybe when the rain lets up, I'll sign your leave." I walked back to my office, grabbed my raincoat and radio, and headed for the motorpool. *Duty calls.*

I stepped outside, tugging at the collar of my yellow slicker. The inside of my van smelled like musty, wet gym socks. A pair of rubber, mud-splattered boots and yellow rain pants lay in a heap on the floorboard. I pulled through the motorpool gate, and stopped where the driveway to the Field Office intersected State Highway 315. I decided to make a detour to the maintenance shop to grab a cup of coffee, before heading out on patrol. The shop always had better coffee. I pulled into the compound and took a side door into the mechanics bay. I walked over to the Bunn, and poured a hefty cup.

I could hear JT cussing creatively. He was searching for something he'd dropped in the engine compartment of a truck he was working on. I walked over to see what all the fuss was about. JT looked up when he saw me come in.

"Dave, you's got skinny white boy fingers. See if you can't grab this damn screw I dropped."

"Only for you, JT."

I set down my coffee, and bent over the grill. Sliding my hand between the engine block and the chassis, I retrieved the screw, and handed it to JT. He beamed.

"I always knew you was good for somethin'."

"JT," I said, taking a sip of coffee, "I'm thinking about getting fixed."

JT surfaced, hitting his head on the hood.

"No, no, no!" he exclaimed. "A man gots to spread his seed."

I'd been thinking about getting fixed for awhile, but was too chickenshit to have someone cut on me down there. *What if a clumsy intern should slip with the scalpel?* JT however, took the whole "go forth and multiply" thing to heart. He was rumored to have fathered dozens of children with different women. I'm not sure I ever believed the stories until they all showed up during one of our Sardis Lake Cleanup Days. In the lead was JT. Strung out behind him were his progeny—nearly two dozen boys and girls of varying heights and ages.

"So, you don't want me to get fixed?" I asked.

"No, sir," JT answered, emphatically.

"I'm just messing with you, JT. I'm not getting fixed."

JT picked up a wrench like he was going to heave it my way, but I was already at the door. I stepped outside. The rain seemed to have let up, but only slightly. I climbed into my van, fired it up, and sat listening to the staccato sounds of windshield wipers backhanding rain...phish-phish, phish-phish, phish-phish. I thought about Logan. I wished I was with him. I stared up at the slate-colored underbellies of some loitering storm clouds, then rolled down the window and stuck out my head.

"Hey," I shouted, "enough with the goddamn rain!"

I rolled up the window, pulled out of the yard, and made my way north, wishing it was Friday.

Not Another Dang Snake Story?

Every great story seems to begin with a snake.
~Nicolas Cage

Ｍay in Mississippi isn't quite the wring-out-your-shirt infernos of July or August, but it's damned hot nonetheless. I stood in a clearing along a dusty road, sweating, and waiting for a yellow school bus to roll up. Behind me, a Cypress swamp teemed with scaled, feathered and furred critters, including a wayward Sasquatch. Well, okay, not a Bigfoot, but maybe a ten pound swamp rabbit? The swamp, and the boardwalk that meandered through it—the Clear Springs Nature Trail—were both named after a nearby spring. Locals often collected the cool, clear spring water to drink and cook with.

I'd discovered the Clear Springs Nature Trail by accident. While returning from a trip to Sardis one afternoon, I saw a faded brown sign indicating a nature trail. I turned off an asphalt road and onto a narrow dirt one, following it until I reached a pullout. And there, in a Mesozoic swamp, were the remnants of a dilapidated boardwalk. Its rotting, mossy floorboards were held skeletally in place by rusty spikes, many of which had worked loose. Entire sections of the boardwalk had collapsed, providing respite for snakes and turtles. The swamp had reclaimed the boardwalk, as a high tide does a sand castle. It was a little like Charlie Brown's Christmas tree… *It's not a bad little boardwalk.*

All it needs is a little fixing up. I presented a proposal to Mr. Walker to rehabilitate the boardwalk. He seemed pleased someone was interested in it, and signed off on the funding.

Work began in the winter (I had to convince the maintenance guys that the snakes were asleep then), and by the following spring, almost a half-mile of boardwalk was complete. The new boardwalk included benches and a large deck for viewing wildlife, and was also handicap accessible. On a scale of one to ten of career accomplishments—where one equals sorting paperclips and ten equals receiving a national award—building the Clear Springs Nature Trail pegged out a solid nine.

#

As the project's Interpretive Services and Outreach Program (ISOP) coordinator, it was my responsibility to schedule school field trips to the Lake. This happened mostly in May, when burned out teachers were on a pedagogical veneer thinner than bargain brand toilet paper. *Please, please, please, Ranger, take my kids, if only for a few hours!* I rarely turned down an educator in need.

On the second Monday in May, right around 10 AM, a long bus with the words "Bramlett Elementary School" stenciled on its side, pulled into the Clear Springs Nature Trail clearing. Dust was on a two second delay. There is no mistaking the excited din of first graders on shore leave. I heard them from a mile off. Probably the whole swamp did.

"Y'all calm down!"

The booming voice with a distinctly Southern punch belonged to my son's first grade teacher. Order was restored, and everyone shuffled off the long bus, and gathered around me. The chaperones brought up the rear. I shifted my Smokey the Bear hat higher onto my head, and looked out on a sea of eager faces.

"Other than having fun," I began, "which is a rule I have, there is only one other rule you must follow. ALWAYS allow the Ranger to go first."

I paused long enough to let that set in, then continued.

"The penalty for breaking this rule is…death!"

The kids gasped in disbelief. Surely the Ranger didn't mean that.

But what if…

I certainly did mean it. A few weeks earlier, I'd met a similar busload of rambunctious youngsters at the Clear Springs trailhead. Interpreters can tell when a teacher has lost control of his or her class. The young woman that climbed off the bus that morning had dark circles pinned under her eyes—the educational equivalent of a combat veteran's 600-yard stare. My mom was an elementary school teacher for twenty years, and some days when she got home, she had that look, especially toward the end of the school year.

Some people would argue, "Well, yeah, but teachers get three months off during the summer." I'd argue, "Well, yeah, but they work their asses off the other nine; coming in early, staying late, loaning lunch money to penniless kids, dealing with dippy parents, recalcitrant school boards, snotty noses, tantrums, bullying, guns, drugs, autism, sexism, racism, and all for shitty pay."

So, on that day, the unruly class and I set off on the boardwalk en masse. No sooner had we stepped onto the boardwalk, when a little boy jolted ahead of me, looking over his shoulder as he ran. Ahead of him, coiled on the boardwalk, was a very robust cottonmouth snake—a common venomous serpent which inhabits swampy areas of the southeastern United States. Cottonmouths are named because of the cottony-white flesh in their mouths. I'd seen my share of cotton in my treks around Sardis Lake, and knew that the snakes can be quite stubborn when it comes to getting out of the way. It's not as if they're lazy snakes; they just pugnaciously stand their ground. From my vantage point twenty feet in arrears, I could tell the snake wasn't going to change its zip code soon. Its tail buzzed loudly on the boardwalk planks, and its mouth was open wide, ready to strike!

"STOP," I bellowed.

Luckily, the snake and the boy obeyed my command. I rushed toward the kid. Our eyes locked. He still had no idea a venomous snake was very close. The serpent belly-flopped off the boardwalk and made a loud cannonball splash, startling the young boy. We peered over the handrail into the pitchy swamp. The snake swam away gracefully, as if performing an aquatic ballet, its massive head riding above the waterline. I placed my hand on the boy's shoulder.

"You almost stepped on a poisonous snake," I said.

He looked up at me, wild-eyed.

"Maybe it's better if I go first."

"...the penalty for breaking this rule is death..."

#

Now, Logan and his class stepped onto the same boardwalk. It meandered through a thick grove of sweet smelling Water Tupelo trees, humming with bees. Bees are nature's matchmakers. They don't have time for romantic candlelight dinners and footsie under the table. With bees, it's gamete to gamete, baby, the original bump and grind. Buzz, buzz, buzz, pollen from the stamen. Buzz, buzz, buzz, rub against the stigma, and BAM, you've got plump Crimson Sweet watermelons, juicy Georgia peaches, crunchy Southern pecans, and of course, Tupelo honey. Van Morrison's bluesy voice echoed in my head...*She's as sweet as Tupelo honey, just like honey from the bee...*

The boardwalk angled out of the Tupelo forest, yielding a panoramic view of the swamp. Fat-bottomed Bald Cypress trees, with their wispy foliage and woody "knees" sticking out of the water, dominated the greenish, duckweed-encrusted waters. A female Wood duck screamed in just below the tree line, attracting the attention of the first graders. For such a beautiful bird, its call sounded more like a wobbly wheel on an ungreased axle. She'd probably just flown the coop, exiting from one of the Wood duck nesting boxes the Corps had placed in the Clear Springs bottomlands.

For weeks, I'd been eyeing one particular nesting box about thirty yards off the boardwalk. Female Wood ducks kept coming and going from it like an avian crack house. Female woodies have been known to dump all their eggs into another nest box. Biologists refer to this as intraspecific brood parasitism. Some other duck mom is left with midnight feedings, baby poop, piano recitals and soccer camps. I suppose it is nature's way of skipping out on motherhood, but for a mamma Wood duck, it's a damn good survival strategy nonetheless. Of course, it's impossible to explain this concept to a horde of first graders that probably needed to pee. Likely, it was *their* moms who packed their lunches, and made sure their socks matched before sending them off to school—not someone else's mom.

When I looked over at the dump box again, I saw something poking out of the entrance hole. It was a large, black rat snake. Rat snakes are excellent climbers. This one had ascended to the Penthouse suite, and likely gorged on complimentary Wood duck eggs. As it crawled down the Cypress tree, I counted six conspicuous bulges, like knots on a counting rope.

I pointed out the snake to the class, and they got very excited as it slalomed through the water, heading toward us. I gave a "Shh" sign, handed over my Ranger hat to a kid, laid down on my stomach, and waited. The children could hardly restrain themselves. The serpent glided under the boardwalk, unaware a crazy Park Ranger waited on the other side. As it swam along unbeknownst, I reached down and plucked it from its morning lap swim. The large rat snake writhed in protest as it was pulled from the swamp. At eye level, the snake's tail tickled the boardwalk. Its cream-colored belly scales shone in the sun. I was concerned the snake might regurgitate its breakfast, but the eggs in its digestive track were more omelet than soft-boiled.

The class, with Logan spearheading the way, circled around me like excited electrons, reaching out with small hands.

"What are those things in the snake?" a little girl asked, pointing to the bulges.

"I think he had some Wood duck eggs for breakfast."

"Eww," she said, withdrawing her hand. There were many more hands to replace hers though.

"Snakes have to eat, too," I said, careful not to sound too sanctimonious. The class crowded around. More questions followed.

"Is it poisonous?"

"What does it eat?"

"Will it bite me?"

"How does it poop?"

I held the Rat snake for awhile, talking about snaky things, as tepid little fingers walked over its scaly back. For some, it may have been their first encounter with a live reptile. I released the snake back into the swamp. We all watched, amazed at the snake's elasticity, as it twisted out of the water like a circus performer, and uncoiled its six foot long body onto a dry log.

We proceeded along the boardwalk until we came upon the wildlife viewing deck. The children checked out the placid swamp waters with newfound curiosity. It wasn't long before shouts rang out.

"There's a turtle!"

"There's a snake!"

"What's that yellow bird?"

"What are those bubbles in the water?"

The whole swamp seemed to be hot-wired, pulsing with life—every aquatic nook and soggy cranny of it. Pond sliders with shiny carapaces took turns climbing on and off a fallen log in conveyor belt fashion. Water snakes shimmied onto small islands to dry out. Ecclesiastical Prothonotary Warblers—their name derived from the bright yellow robes that clerks in the Roman Catholic Church wear—flitted about, scissoring beetles and caterpillars with their pointy beaks. Underneath the inky water, in the organic, oozy bowels of the swamp, anaerobic bacteria feasted on the carcasses of plants and animals, forming methane, nitrogen and other gases, which bubbled to the surface like Alka-Seltzer.

We continued walking on the boardwalk until it reunited with dry land, then traipsed under a shady canopy of mature poplars, beeches, oaks and gum trees until we came to a dirt road. For the last half mile back to the bus, we walked single-file. When I looked over my shoulder, Logan was scampering in and out of a marshy ditch that paralleled the road, probably hoping to catch an unsuspecting bullfrog or a lazy garter snake. I smiled. *Someday, that boy will make a fine Ranger.*

Finally, we arrived where we started. The bus driver, an older black man, leaned against the grill of the yellow school bus, arms folded. He smiled as I approached.

"See's any snakes?" he asked.

"Yessir, sure did."

I took off my hat and wiped my brow. The weather had turned noticeably muggier. Rain was coming.

"See's any hoop snakes?" the bus driver asked.

I looked at him. His large hands suggested he was no stranger to hard work. No doubt, he'd encountered snakes in the wild. *But a Hoop Snake?*

"What is a hoop snake?" I asked, feeling like a bass with a hook in its lip. He unfolded his arms, and started talking about working in the hill country of Tishomingo County, in northeastern Mississippi.

"I'm cuttin' pulpwood, and on the ground is a big snake just layin' there."

"Yeah?" I said, curious.

"Well, the snake sees me comin' and grabs at its tail." With this, he creates a round O, with his arms held high over his head.

"Then the snake starts to rollin' down the hill. Slow at first. Rolls over rocks, stumps, don't matter, just keeps rollin,' faster and faster down the hill. Sure enough!" I pictured a runaway hula-hoop.

"So, that's why you call it a hoop-snake?"

He walked around the bus, and climbed up into the driver's seat.

"I reckon, yessir," he said, smiling.

I felt a distinct tug. *Reeled in, hook, line and sinker!*

A light drizzle began falling. Logan's teacher tried in vain to protect her bouffant coiffure, using her hands as a crude umbrella. She clearly wasn't enjoying her outing to Sardis Lake much. I felt sorry for her. Perhaps an art museum was more to her liking.

#

As with the bus driver's hoop snake story, everyone, it seems, has a snake story to tell. Not sure everyone has a hamster story in their repertoire, though. Growing up, we had a pet hamster named Sally. She was portly, whiskery and a notorious finger biter. One day, Sally escaped her cage, and sought refuge in the recesses of the family sofa. Her escape did not go unnoticed by the family dog, Cubby, who eviscerated the Naugahyde couch trying to eat her. Polyfill blanketed the family room like snow. Dad practically had an aneurism. I thought it was curtains for Cubby, who stood shoulder deep in microfibers, panting like a bellows, wagging his shaggy, black tail. I can't recall if Sally ever surfaced again. But if we had a snake loose in the house, it might've quietly dispatched Sally, thereby saving the couch from its confettied demise.

My octogenarian mom, now a widow, leaves a pair of men's work boots on the front porch. When I asked her why, she said it keeps thieves away. Would-be criminals, after seeing a pair of size twelve boots, might conclude there's a big man in the house, and take a pass on robbing the place. I told her she just needed to pin a note on the door:

George, the damn snake is loose in the house again!!

No burglar would have the balls.

The bus driver fired up the bus, and as I was wrapping things up, a kid in the back of the bus blurted out, "There's a snake!" Everyone shifted to his side of the bus to have a look. The teacher however, gravitated to the other.

I looked through the driver's side window. In a clearing just off the port bow, was a magnificent black racer. I walked off the bus and into a light rain. Looking over my shoulder, I saw children's faces pressed against the bus windows.

Racers generally have an ornery disposition, and strike whenever the opportunity arises. They're equipped with sharp, curved teeth which they use to effectively grab their prey. I reached for the racer's slippery tail and missed, badly. The snake whipped around and clamped down on my forearm. I turned my back to the bus, so the kids couldn't see, and with my free hand, extracted the racers' teeth from my arm. Pinpricks of blood bubbled to the surface, revealing a crimson horseshoe pattern. I headed back to the bus holding my wiggling prize, which could have stretched across the hood of the bus. I wiped blood on my pants before boarding.

I started down the aisle with the sleek racer, so that all the children could have an opportunity to touch it. Logan's teacher was plastered to the back of the school bus, right under the Emergency Exit sign. Her face was contorted, like a scream queen in a B-horror flick. Short of bolting out a window, which she looked willing to do, the poor woman had no place to hide. I quickly about-faced and walked toward the front of the bus, Mr. Racer held high. Excited first graders followed me off the bus and into the clearing where I caught him (or he caught me). I placed the racer on the ground, and with one kinetic flex, he shot across the clearing, spiraled up a hickory sapling, and peered back at us. *See you next time, buddy.*

#

If you walk into any pet store, it's a good bet you'll see puppies with Hershey kisses eyes, begging you to take them home, or kittens meowing lissomly, pawing at their glass enclosures. You probably won't see families lined up checking out Eyelash Crested Geckos or Ball Pythons. I get it. Reptiles are as far from cuddly as Andy Kaufman was from being a wrestler. Snakes lie on their hot rocks and stare impassively. They don't give a shit.

On the Clear Springs Boardwalk that day though, the kids were eager to touch the Rat snake I'd plucked from the swamp. Curiosity supplanted fear. Humans don't come out of the womb hating reptiles; they *learn* it. At some point in her life, Logan's teacher might've had a psyche-searing snake experience, after which she could no more cozy up to a snake than a surfer could to a shark. Sadly, she is not alone in that regard.

\#

About a week after the Clear Springs Nature Trial outing, a large, manila envelope addressed to Ranger Dave, arrived at the Sardis Lake Field Office. The return address read:

Bramlett Elementary School
Oxford, Mississippi

I opened the envelope. Out spilled a potpourri of crayon Picassos, all beautifully rendered on blue-lined, first grade stationary. There were pictures of a stick-figured Ranger holding a crooked black rod (snake?), and wearing a big hat that looked like something Hoss Cartwright wore. Many of the pictures had heartfelt renderings of their outing to Sardis Lake, "We Love Snakes!" It was first grader fan mail—the kind a Ranger keeps squirreled away in a desk drawer, and occasionally pulls out and looks at when they're having an especially cocked up day. I was enjoying the pictures, when Louise stepped into my office, holding a 32-ounce Diet Coke.

"The Rangers were trying to get you on the radio," she said, sipping her drink through a red straw. I looked at the radio cradle on my desk.

"Sorry, my radio was charging. What did they want?"

"It was Percy Bruce goin' on about a snake wrapped around the axle of his truck up in Hipps Hollow. I think he wants you to git it off."

I put the fan mail back into a drawer, collected my radio and headed for the door.

Go West, Middle-Aged Man!

And so by the fifteenth century, on October 8, the
Europeans were looking for a new place to try to get to,
and they came up with a new concept: the West.
~Dave Barry

In the fall of 1998, Kate came home from school and proudly announced she was "fixin' to do her homework." Mary B and I looked at each other, dumfounded. She'd never talked that way before. At this point, we'd lived in Mississippi for twelve years. Oxford was to be our way station, a stopover in the terminal of life. It had turned into an extended layover. Mississippi would never be our home, we both knew that. At the end of the day, Mary B and I were two lost Californians, adrift in a sea of RC Colas and Moon Pies.

When we left Mammoth Cave, our plan was to head south, get a promotion, and hopefully relocate out west. The promotion part of the plan worked well enough—I'd moved up the Government Standard (GS) food chain from a GS-5 to a GS-9—but the moving west part laid in tatters in a drainage ditch along I-55, somewhere south of Memphis.

Yet Mississippi wasn't all gloom and doom, in fact, far from it. At the risk of sounding like a Christmas letter—the one you unfailingly get every year from those special relatives who vacation in the Azores, whose grandchildren solve differential calculus equations, and whose Floribunda Rose won Best of Show at the State Fair, again—at the risk of sounding like them, I'll give the Dutton drum a few whacks.

Kate turned out to be an industrious Girl Scout. Each year at cookie time, our living room filled up with boxes of Samoas, Tagalongs, Trefoils, and Thin Mints. What we didn't eat, we sold. She joined the local swim club. After work, the kids and I often walked two blocks to the city pool for a refreshing dip. Most of the pools in Oxford were exclusive, or had exorbitant membership fees. At the city pool though, we could swim all day for pocket change, and have enough leftover for a candy bar and slurpee at the snack stand.

Logan discovered everything in our wooded backyard that hopped, crawled, slithered or flew. He joined a youth soccer league, and played on a team that won a city championship. His coach—an eccentric fellow with a passion for all things Italian—nicknamed him *Lego Logano*, partly because of Logan's fetish for Legos.

Mary B and I waded into the community waters too. As co-PTA Presidents, we organized book fairs, browbeat parents into volunteering for school beautification projects, and hocked overpriced candy bars outside the Piggy Wiggly, to raise money to buy books for the school library. We became active in the swim club, and even studied to become "stroke and turn" judges, although I never could bring myself to disqualify a swimmer.

Career-wise, things were pretty peachy as well. In 1995, the US Army Corps of Engineers bestowed upon me the first ever "Interpreter of the Year" award. I was selected from a nationwide cadre of talented Corps Park Rangers. The whole family traveled to Washington, D.C. for the award ceremony. We bunked in a fancy hotel that left mints on our pillows at nighttime, and I got an opportunity to hobnob with Corps top brass, including the *Jefe* himself—The Chief of the Corps of Engineers. He presented me with the Hiram M. Chittenden Award for Interpretive Excellence. My fifteen minutes of fame warranted a full paragraph in the Dutton Christmas letter that year. My mom even badgered the editor of my hometown newspaper, the Record-Ledger, to run a story about her son's achievement.

The reality though, was that Oxford—the bucolic southern small town that William Faulkner once roamed (presumably without his BVDs)—began showing signs of what Stephen King or Peter Straub called *slippage*. Oxford's slippage was brought on by the town's elders selling their souls to the Beelzebub of "managed growth." It reminded me of Edward Abbey, author, and passionate advocate of the American West, who once opined, "Growth for the sake of growth is a cancerous madness." In the early 90s, Oxford needed hefty doses of chemotherapy!

Developers began pushing over, leveling and carting away the city's iconic hardwood forests by the metric ton, presumably to make room for more condos, big box stores and parking lots. Regal oaks—some perhaps old enough to have fathered acorns during the battles of Antietam and Shiloh—were sacrificed in the name of "managed growth."

Nowhere in Oxford though, were the effects of the cities' pro-growth policies more on display than the widening of West Jackson Avenue—an east-west thoroughfare through town. During one raucous Town Hall meeting, attended by angry, pitchfork-carrying citizens, the city council voted to widen the avenue. It was a close vote, but it was also a death knell for shady Oxford. The citizenry, pissed and frothing, rose up defiantly. Mr. Abbey would've been proud. The battle lines were drawn—environmentally conscious Oxonians vs. well-financed developers. But it was more than a David versus Goliath struggle. The town's money interests were far too entrenched; the "tree-huggers" never stood a chance.

After the fateful decision was cast to widen West Jackson Avenue, Mary B rose up and angrily stabbed her finger at the smug aldermen sitting in their overstuffed chairs. An election was coming soon, and many of the aldermen who voted to widen West Jackson were up for reelection.

"We will vote you out!" she hissed at them.

Soon, the Caterpillars came, the backhoes and the frontend loaders too. Diesel fouled the air. With the machines, came the protesters. I never really thought myself a "tree-hugger," yet there

I was, squatting with eight other like-minded people under the crown of a massive Red oak, staring down a belching D-9 dozer intent on toppling the tree, like a spare. Our sit-in drew cheers of solidarity from the gathering throngs. It also drew the attention of the Oxford PD.

Police cars with flashing blue lights soon pulled up to the construction site. Policemen rushed out, batons and pepper spray at the ready. One by one, Oxford's finest culled us from the protesting herd, cuffed us, placed us in squad cars, and hauled us away to jail. We were fingerprinted, photographed, and thrown into holding cells. Somewhere in the archives of the Oxford City Police Department, there are pictures of a bearded Park Ranger holding a placard, looking left, looking right, looking straight.

Later that afternoon, they released us. A cop gave me a ride home, and as we drove, he told me he was with us in spirit and didn't agree with what the city was doing. But he wore a badge and had to do what his superiors told him to do. I got out of the squad car, and leaned into the open window.

"Just because you wear a uniform," I told him, "doesn't mean you have to check your first amendment rights at the door." The former director of the National Park Service once told me that, and it seemed like the perfect thing to say at the time. I felt like a poet. The cop smiled and drove off.

The front page headline in the *Oxford Eagle* the next day dubbed us the "Oxford-9." We were arraigned in front of a magistrate judge. The eyes of a packed courtroom were upon us. I wore a tie. The judge, an elected official, weighed his options. Most of the people in his courtroom were not advocates of widening West Jackson, and he knew it.

As it turned out, we were arrested on University of Mississippi property. Oxford PD had no jurisdiction there, so we were all given "Get out of Jail Free" cards. Outside the courthouse, there was a lot of back-slapping and high-fiving. Although we weren't going to be jailbirds, we also knew our actions hadn't done squat to curb the "managed growth" still raging around town.

Fortunately however, there was one place that hadn't yet been touched by the cudgel of progress. It was a small pond, situated in a low area between a gas station and a motel, on the far end of town. The Dutton family made yearly pilgrimages to it in the spring. With the exception of an occasional Cheetos bag or Slurpee cup floating in the pond, the place was a jewel. Spring peepers—those amphibious harbingers of spring—congregated there to raucously procreate. It was our springtime nirvana. Some nights, the decibel level around the pond rivaled a Deep Purple concert. Kate plugged her ears with tiny fingers, while her brother shined his flashlight across the pond, looking for glistening, bulbous eyes just above the waterline.

One muggy spring evening following a soft rain—ripe conditions for peeper love—we excitedly grabbed our flashlights and drove across town to the pond. We got out, bracing for an audible assault, yet it was eerily silent...no amps...no wailing guitars. Logan switched on his flashlight first. His D-cell light report did not include sightings of iridescent Peeper eyes; neither did mine. Mary's and Kate's also reported nothing. Instead, our beams arced across lifeless, ebony asphalt, lined with white, parallel parking stripes. Logan walked to where the pond used to be, staring in disbelief. Kate pulled her fingers from her ears. The place of the tiny amphibians was no more. It had been paved over. We got back in the van, mired in ugly thoughts. On the drive home, Mary B touched me on the arm.

"Ranger," she said in a hushed tone, "we need to go. We need to leave Oxford."

Dashboard lights glimmered in her eyes. I knew exactly what she meant. It was just a shitty little pond, but it was always *our* shitty little pond. I wanted to leave Oxford behind and drive west until the rising sun warmed our backs. I wanted to drive until I was back in the land of iconic mesas, where I could get a decent breakfast burrito obscenely smothered in red chile. It was time to leave Oxford. We both knew that. *Someday Ol' Man River, you're gonna be in my rearview mirror.*

About six months after we discovered the peepers had been forcibly evicted, I turned on my computer at work, and an odd email popped up on the screen:

From: DOUGLAS R BAILEY at CESPA-OD-CH
To: LMKDM C.SLFO (DAVE_DUTTON)
Date: 9/5/98 9:05am
Subject: GS-11 Lead Ranger Cochiti Lake

This will confirm that if selected that yes you do want to come.

The reason or reasons for the decision I understand are many.

How would you describe you management style?

How do you work with ethnic diversity?

Thanks – Douglas

Douglas was the Operations Manager at Cochiti Lake, New Mexico. In my Westward-ho quest the previous July, I'd responded to vacancy announcement KS98-187, GS-11 Park Ranger, Cochiti Lake. I hadn't heard a peeper since. I'd sent in my SF-171 and KSA's (Remember those?). After three months of not hearing anything, I figured I was out of the running for the job. Now, apparently, I wasn't.

#

In the fall of 1982, when Mary B and I lived at Bandelier, we descended out of the Jemez Mountains, and briefly visited Cochiti Dam—a massive Corps of Engineers earthen structure stretched out before the Rio Grande. We were on our way to Dixon's apple orchard a few miles upstream of Cochiti Lake. As we drove by the dam, I felt dwarfed, like sitting in a dingy docked alongside the Queen Mary. I also recall how barren and lifeless the place looked.

"I'm glad you don't work here," Mary B said, unimpressed.

#

September 1998 at Sardis Lake came and went. As I waited for Mother Nature to trip the cool switch, more emails from the mysterious Mr. Douglas surfaced on my computer. I promptly responded to all his queries. *Was I being interviewed for the Cochiti position via email?*

On October 8—the same day historian Dave Barry posited that Europeans discovered the West—I got my answer. An HR specialist in the South Pacific Division Office of the Corps of Engineers called me. I found it puzzling that the Albuquerque District Corps of Engineers, located in the middle of a desert, was part of the South Pacific Division. The nice lady informed me I'd been selected for the Lead Ranger position at Cochiti Lake. She asked if I was still interested in the job. As cool as James Bond ordering a martini, I replied, "I'd like to talk this over with my wife first. Can I get back to you tomorrow?"

"Yes, of course," she said.

I hung up the phone and rushed down the hall to Billie Lee's office, leave slip in hand, then sped home to Oxford.

I walked into the kitchen and announced, "Mary B, pack your bags. We're fixin' to move west!"

She hugged me as tight as when we found out we were moving to Kentucky, then added, "We'll have to tell the kids."

#

After I accepted the Senior Ranger position at Cochiti Lake, our lives began whirling faster than a blender at Orange Julius. I asked Mr. Bailey, my new boss, if I could start at Cochiti after the holidays. He agreed. All we needed to do before then was fly my mother-in-law out to Mississippi to babysit the kids while we house-hunted in New Mexico, put our own house on the market, sell it, pack and move west 1,100 miles. In between, we'd celebrate Christmas. Easy peasy.

The week before Thanksgiving, Mary and I boarded a plane in Memphis, and touched down in Albuquerque. The last time we saw Albuquerque, Mary B, Daniel and I were heading east to Mammoth Cave. We got a rental car and headed north up I-25, admiring the snow-dusted peaks of the Sangre de Cristo Mountains, which sheltered Santa Fe. To the west was the great Rio Grande Rift—a massive continental shift that allowed the Rio Grande to flow all the way to the Gulf of Mexico. Just up the Interstate was Cochiti Dam.

We turned off the highway, and followed the signs for Cochiti Lake. We drove down to the boat ramp, got out, and marveled at the placid waters of the Rio Grande. The air was suffused with juniper and sage. A white gull winged over a glassy lake, looking at its reflection as it flew. Overhead, scant white puffs floated in an indigo sky. We stood on the shoreline for twenty minutes, holding hands, not saying a word. Then, we hopped in the rental and headed to Santa Fe—the City Different.

When we weren't house hunting, Mary B and I strolled about Santa Fe's historic plaza, admiring the Spanish architecture and Native American crafts. We sucked in enough Piñon-laden air to fill a hot air balloon. I ate chile with an "e" at every meal, though I paid a steep price at the pump because of it. In the evenings, I washed chile down with liberal amounts of blue agave, or sponged it up with a sopaipilla—a doughy concoction of flour, deep-fried to a pillowy consistency.

We placed a successful bid on a house in a Santa Fe subdivision. The realtor told us that a couple from Texas, who were out of the country at the time, planned to buy the house when they got back. Not finance it, mind you, buy it outright, like buying a house in Monopoly. We'd beaten them to the punch.

After our successful house hunting trip, we hurried back to Oxford. I spent the next two weeks trying to tie up loose ends at work. After a dozen years of rangering at the Sardis Lake Field Office, it wasn't easy. One morning, after I got back to the office, Louise greeted me in the hallway.

"Mr. Walker wants to see you in the conference room ASAP," she said. *Not sure this is good.*

My apprehension dissolved when I pushed opened the conference room door, and saw it packed with familiar faces—volunteers I'd worked with during my tenure at Sardis Lake. Ms. Wingo smiled as she saw the surprise on my face. She was the reason they were all gathered. She'd rung them up. I was sure of it. Mr. Walker stood in the front of the conference room, beckoning me in with his large hands.

The Mayor of Sardis was in the room. He stood first and read aloud a proclamation that culminated with NOW THEREFORE, I, Ernest L. Scruggs, Mayor of the City of Sardis, do proclaim this, the FIFEENTH day of DECEMBER, 1998, as "RANGER DAVE DAY." I was floored. I'd never had a day named after me.

Another longtime Sardis Lake volunteer who was also a Mississippi State legislator read aloud a framed commendation: NOW, THEREFORE, *We do hereby commend Ranger David Dutton for his dedicated and exemplary service to the citizens of Mississippi.* Later, he pulled me aside and told me I was in tall cotton because Archie Manning—the legendary All-American quarterback from Ole Miss—also had a plaque like mine. *This puppy's goin' on the wall!*

Ms. Wingo came up to me afterwards and gave me a big hug. "You've earned this, Mr. Dutton," she said with a hard smile. "We will miss you."

That afternoon I drove home with a head so swollen, there was hardly room in the van for the rest of me. I was going to miss the volunteers I'd worked so closely with during my time at the Sardis Lake Field Office, especially Ms. Wingo. It was she who'd forged the foundations for successful public outreach and citizen involvement at Sardis Lake. Frankly, all I did was drive the bus.

#

To help sell our house, we enlisted the help of Mr. Walker's wife, Gwen, who was a successful Oxford realtor. Her effervescence rivaled that of club soda. We reeled in an excellent catch on the house with our first cast, selling it in just one day. Things were looking "finer than frog hair," as my southern colleagues might say.

As Christmas 1998 approached, I ventured onto Corps property, axe in hand, and cut down what would be our last Christmas tree in Mississippi. When I dragged it home, and set it in the stand however, the tree was rounder than Alfred Hitchcock in side profile. We called it, "The Christmas Bush." I was in a yuletide slump; 0 for 17 in spatially arranging Christmas trees in an appropriate interior setting.

St. Nick and his reindeer landed on our front lawn again, stripping lichens from our Cypress tree, again. We didn't have a chimney, so the jolly man brought his goodies through the front door, which was always unlocked on Christmas Eve. Each year I told the kids that Santa's reindeer would be hungry, and that they especially favored lichens. On Christmas morn, most kids would rush out to see what Santa had left under the Christmas Bush. Mine however, bolted out the front door, intent on inspecting the Cypress tree for evidence of reindeer snacking. Poor kids. It wasn't their fault they had a naturalist, and part-time Santa, as a Dad.

#

After Christmas, I traveled south to Jackson to pick up my younger brother, Paul, at the airport. At 6'4" and 220 pounds, I couldn't really call him my little brother. Paul had volunteered to come out to Mississippi, and help us drive one of our two vans (yes, we were a two-van family), out to New Mexico.

A few days after Christmas, a moving van pulled curbside to our house on North 9th Street. Uniformed men stuffed our stuff into cardboard boxes, and then stuffed the boxes into a cavernous truck. By day's end, they'd loaded almost nine tons of household stuff. It was a far cry from the 140 cubic feet of space we needed when we moved to Bandelier. *How'd we collect so much stuff?* We would've exceeded eighteen thousand pounds too, except the lawnmower got left behind. Where we were going, people didn't have grass lawns, or if they did, they were only big enough to dance half a Polka on.

We spent our last night in Oxford in the same place where we spent our first night in Oxford—the Holiday Inn. Except this time, we had two children, two guppies, and only *one* dog.

I think it was George Carlin who said, "Life is a series of dogs." A sad metric if ever there was one, but true nonetheless. Gone from our life was Daniel, the German shepherd with a penchant for gourmet jelly beans—the dog who crapped on every byway in Texas, when we journeyed east to Kentucky in 1983. Daniel never asked for anything, except an occasional sausage link from Denny's or a pat on the head. He was at the door when we brought Kate home from the hospital. He took his diminished status in the household pecking order graciously; protecting Kate as she slept on the floor between his big furry legs in her footie pajamas.

It was gut-wrenching to watch Mary B say goodbye to her companion of fifteen years. Daniel's furry ears sponged up her tears. *She's losing her baby.* I walked Daniel to the car and helped him into the back seat. His hips had lost their bounce. The ride to the vet's office was somber. Daniel looked out the window at anemic Bradford pear trees along West Jackson Avenue. Gone were the regal oaks, whose glorious crowns once shaded the road.

In the vet's office, I stroked Daniel's thick fur, trying to hold it together as the pentobarbital coursed through his veins. He closed his eyes, and then it was done. I walked out to the car, and rested my forehead on the steering wheel, sobbing with a fury that rocked the van. When I got home, Cinnamon and I locked eyes. Mine were bloodshot, his worried. He knew his old friend would never be coming home again.

A couple of years later, I was in the same vet's office. This time, I stroked Cinnamon's toasted marshmallow-colored fur. As I watched him drift away, his nose gave one last twitch.

"You back in Kentucky chasin' down fat toads, boy?" Cinnamon didn't answer. *Rest in peace, toad snifter.*

\#

After Daniel passed, our hearts were on our shoelaces. Mary B and I traveled a hundred miles north, to Millington, Tennessee, and shelled out $150 for a German shepherd puppy. I'd never spent that much money on an animal before in my life. We called him Dillon, and he was a wildling. He'd perfected a crazy maneuver we called slam dancin'. He'd run pell-mell and slide on the kitchen linoleum like Pete Rose stealing second base, careening into the walls, sometimes knocking picture frames from their hooks.

Dillon grew into a magnificent specimen. By the time of our move west in 1998 though, he was getting senior in the dog calculus. His once dark muzzle was peppered with gray, and he began preferring softer things to rest his bones on. And so it was Dillon who shared our last night in Oxford with us. And, like Daniel before him, he would take in the vastness of the plains, only he would see them with the rising sun in his eyes.

\#

It's approximately 1,062 miles from Sardis Lake, Mississippi, to Santa Fe, New Mexico—not including the mile detour we made to the Beacon Restaurant on the morning of our departure. There's nothing like an artery-clogging breakfast of biscuits and gravy, butter-lavished grits and a side of crispy bacon, to kick off a road trip. Wash it all down with a cup of black coffee and I'm good for 400 miles.

Road Axiom #3: Although the notion that your bladder shrinks with age is medical bootsey, it is a fact that the older you get, the more piss breaks you require.

Mary B, Logan, Kate, Dillon, brother Paul, two guppies, and I, all pushed away from the Beacon Restaurant in two bulging minivans. By the time we reached Memphis an hour later, the oblique winter sun had warmed things enough so that we could drive with the windows down. I smelled the fecund Mississippi River, and the succulent aromas of Memphis BBQ. Suddenly, I had a hankerin' for a pulled pork sandwich.

We followed a dizzying array of green and white Interstate signs, making ballsy lane changes, until we reached the Memphis-Arkansas Memorial Bridge. It was our conduit west. We drove over the bridge. Far below was the gumbo-colored Mississippi— the "Big Muddy,"—a river that shunted water from as far away as New Mexico, a state still 1,000 miles west. *Ol' Man River is finally at my back!*

We caravanned west along I-40. With each passing mile, the sounds coming out of Rock 103, WEGR, a popular FM Memphis rock station, grew fainter and fainter. While on Ranger patrols at Sardis Lake, I often listened to Rock 103. It was the kind of station where the deejays played Skynyard's "Freebird" to the very last chord, then punctuated the song with a throaty exhortation..."Yeahhhhhhh!"

Throughout the day we raced the sun west, steadily losing ground, until we peeked at its last rays from behind our visors. We pulled into a Motel 6 on the outskirts of Oklahoma City. Tom Bodett was gracious enough to leave the light on for us.

The next morning we rose early, and after a robust Waffle House breakfast, set off into the wind-whipped Great Plains— two Dodge schooners racing across the prairie. Santa Fe awaited us at the terminus of the Rocky Mountains, 500 miles to the west. We motored through the Texas panhandle, and Dillon, just like Daniel, unleashed a shit storm. *Texas just brings out the best in dogs, I suppose.*

Shadows were growing long when we crossed into New Mexico. A large, yellow billboard greeted us. It read:

Welcome to

N E W M E X I C O
The Land of Enchantment

Two chile peppers, one red, one green, adorned the upper left corner of the yellow billboard.

We gassed up the ponies in Tucumcari, grabbed some stale corn nuts and burnt coffee, and some high fructose corn syrup snacks for the kids, and continued our gallop west. At a funky crossroads called Clines Corners, we exited the interstate and headed north. Two hours later, five road-weary humans, one cold German shepherd, and two guppies, pulled into the parking lot of the Inn of the Governors in downtown Santa Fe.

I stepped out of the van and stretched, exorcising knotty demons that'd possessed my back since Amarillo. Overhead, the Milky Way twinkled, and in the frigid mountain air, I could see every one of its 300 billion stars. I admired the glowing holiday farolitos that lined the parapet walls of the three-story hotel. Colorful twined strands of red chile peppers dangled from portals and vigas. Piñon smoke wafted from kiva fireplaces. I checked us in, and we all scurried upstairs to warm rooms, clutching our free breakfast coupons.

Early the next morning, I was awakened by the tinny jingling of dog tags. Dillon paced the room. He had business to transact. I did too. The two of us stepped out onto the balcony. Icy fuzz grew everywhere. From the second story I could see the snow-glazed Sangre de Cristo Mountains glowing in the day's first light. Dillon yanked me down two flights of frosty stairs to the parking lot. I remembered I needed something from the van, which resembled a frosty Bon-Bon. I slid the side door open. The fish!

In the hubbub of getting checked in the night before, I'd completely forgotten about the little guppies. I reached down and cupped the frozen glass bowl in my palms. Two guppies stared back. They reminded me of the victims of Pompeii, except ice, not fiery ash caused their death. How was I going to tell Kate her beloved guppies became ice cubes?

As it turned out, science was the answer. I sat Kate down and told her about the strange properties of water, how it freezes from the top down. Normally, this allows fish to swim under the ice I explained, but in the case of her guppies, there wasn't enough water in the bowl, so it all turned to ice. It was a lie whiter than any Sears appliance, but Kate took it well. Of course, the truth was the guppies had suffocated from lack of oxygen. *But hey, what sounds worse: death by suffocation or freezing to death?*

#

On January 1, 1999, I rose early and dressed in the dark. I opened a plastic pouch of tasteless hotel room coffee, poured in cold water, flipped a switch, and waited for dark liquid to fill a small glass urn. I put on a heavy jacket, poured the coffee into a travel mug, grabbed my Santa Fe ball cap, and stepped into a sub-freezing morning. Clouds of miniscule ice crystals flitted in the morning air like pixie dust. I made my way to the van, hopped onto an icy bucket seat, and turned the ignition. The car sputtered, sending cold, viscous oil through its steely vesicles. I turned on the defroster, sipped the Arabica bean, and waited as the minivan slowly lost its freezer patina.

The sun had barely crested the horizon as the van and I chugged up the volcanic flanks of an ancient, bowl-shaped caldera, enroute to Los Alamos, New Mexico. The road switch-backed higher and higher, through a landscape of pinkish, pockmarked rocks ensconced in snow and ice. The sun felt plenary radiating through the windshield.

I turned onto NM 4, then again onto the entrance road for Bandelier National Monument. I drove past an adobe entrance station, and stopped at a gate. I wasn't sure if the monument would be open on New Year's Day. Then I saw parallel tire prints in the snow on the opposite side of the gate. *It's unlocked.* I opened the gate, pulled through, closed it behind me, and proceeded on.

The icy road clung to a mesa and went by the fire tower where I spent my first summer at Bandelier, before making a sweeping arc and descending into a spectacular canyon. I could see the Rio Grande far below, shimmering in the morning's first light. I followed the lone set of tire tracks deeper into the canyon until the road flattened out into a small, oval parking lot flanked by old rock buildings with pointy timbers sticking out of them near the roofline.

I parked next to the Visitor Center and got out. *Has it really been twenty years since I first walked through its doors?* A pickup truck with a camper shell was parked outside the VC. Footprints in the snow led away from the building. I followed them like Inspector Clouseau, only without his iconic magnifying glass.

The tracks meandered along a trail bordering Frijoles Creek. I continued up the trail, and crossed a narrow footbridge. Midway across the bridge, I stopped and looked down. Sitting on a snow bank below, with her feet in the creek, was Kristen—my first supervisor. Her long brown hair had faded some, but, unlike my own, lacked any gray. We both looked like we'd had a few too many slices of birthday cake over the years.

"I guess they've eased the standards to be in the Polar Bear Club these days," I said, shattering the wintry stillness. Kristen looked up, startled. She studied the bearded man on the bridge for a moment.

"Dave Dutton," she said, smiling, "I didn't expect to see you here."

"Neither did I."

I worked my way down to the bank and sat in the snow next to her. I took off my boots and socks and plunged my feet into the water, feeling its icy piercings. Two former Polar Bear Club alumni sat side-by-side, not saying a word. The murmuring creek eddied around our white ankles. A light canyon breeze blew the crowns of Ponderosa pines, relieving snow-laden boughs of their wet burdens. Water and wind—the only sounds in the world. I closed my eyes and breathed deep, filling my lungs with sweet, crisp mountain air. It smelled right.

I'm home.

68078914R00115

Made in the USA
Charleston, SC
02 March 2017